# In Context

## Language and drama in the secondary school

John Seely

Head of English and drama
The Knights Templar
School, Baldock

Oxford University Press 1976

Oxford University Press, Ely House, London W1

*Glasgow New York Toronto Melbourne Wellington*
*Cape Town Ibadan Nairobi Dar es Salaam Lusaka Addis Ababa*
*Delhi Bombay Calcutta Madras Karachi Lahore Dacca*
*Kuala Lumpur Singapore Hong Kong Tokyo*

Printed in Great Britain by
J. W. Arrowsmith Ltd.,
Bristol

For Edith and Austin

# Acknowledgements

This book is the product of practical work in a number of different educational environments, and without the enthusiastic support of students and pupils in different parts of the country, it would never have been written. I am particularly grateful to my pupils at the Knights Templar School, Baldock, who tried many of the ideas out, and especially to Darrel, Janette, Angela, Stephen, Richard, Chris, and the other members of the 1972—5 special drama group, for all their hard work. On the theoretical side, I am indebted to Desmond Vowles of the Reading University School of Education, to Martin Davies of Stirling University, and to Geraint Lloyd-Evans, Hertfordshire English Adviser, for much helpful criticism and advice while the book was in preparation. Finally, the whole project would have been impossible without the encouragement and practical involvement of my wife, Elizabeth.

# Contents

Author

Title        In context

Stock no. 5713436

This item should be returned or brought in for renewal
by the last date stamped below

19 APR. 1982

20. FEB. 1986

31. OCT. 1986

18 MAR 1988

13. JUN. 1989

19. MAR. 1992

27. MAY 1992

-3. NOV. 1992

24. JUN. 1993

-3. DEC. 1993

10. JAN. 1994

21. FEB. 1994

25. MAR. 1994

-2. DEC. 1994

26. MAY 1995

Welsh College of Music and Drama, Castle Grounds,
Cathays Park, Cardiff, CF1 3ER

4/80 GP00147KRS PPP

Contents

Contents

# Introduction:
# drama, language, and teachers

'Drama' is a word that arouses many and conflicting emotions when it crops up in the secondary school staffroom. It does this whether one is talking to a drama specialist or to a teacher of another subject, to a headmaster or a head of English. It behoves the writer of a book on the subject, therefore, to be very clear both about the precise nature of his subject-matter and about the readership for whom it is intended. To begin rather negatively, this is not a book about drama in general, nor is it primarily intended for drama specialists. Rather, it concerns that area of educational drama that has come to be known as 'improvisation': an activity in which the children are given (or invent) characters, relationships, place, and time, and then act through a scene or situation using speech and movement, but without any detailed or preconceived plan or script. It is written for the kind of teacher I have often spoken to in secondary schools who begins a sentence with 'I'd like to do some drama, but . . .' These have mostly been English teachers, but the need can also be felt by teachers of other subjects.

But what? If one examines some of the possible continuations of that sentence one can perhaps discover some of the requirements that a book about improvisation needs to satisfy if it is to be useful.

'I'd like to do some drama, but . . .
1 . . . I'm worried about discipline.'
2 . . . the headmaster complains if there's too much noise.'
3 . . . I don't feel confident to.'
4 . . . I haven't got time.'
5 . . . I don't know where to begin.'
6 . . . once I've begun I don't know how to progress.'

The problems implied here are concerned with three main areas:
    rationale
    practical applications
    the school context in which drama takes place.

1

The problem has always been that while it is possible to direct the enquiring teacher to books that will deal with the first category and others that try to deal with the second, there are very few that tackle the third and apparently none that produce a completely satisfactory blend of all three—at least as far as the secondary school is concerned.

The situation is made worse by the lack of agreement about what the word 'drama' really means. There is no 'progressive consensus'[1] here to compare with that which can just about be distinguished in the much broader field of English teaching. Different writers and practitioners say different things. This would be all very well if every school had its own department, or at least specialist. If there were no agreement about what teachers of art were supposed to be doing, at least there are enough of them in most schools to get on and do it: the work does not have to be done by teachers of other subjects. Yet this is precisely the situation with drama. Relatively few schools have on their staffs trained drama specialists teaching only or mainly drama, and in most secondary schools where drama is taught the work is done by teachers whose main professional qualifications and preoccupations remain elsewhere.

This confusion reflects the eclectic (I nearly wrote 'schizophrenic') nature of educational drama in its broadest applications: its activities range from movement and dance, where it merges with physical education, to concern with text, which links it with English. In a sense a large confidence trick has been played on the educational system whereby a subject has been 'invented' and people trained to teach it, but schools in general have not found room for it on a similar scale. Teachers have been left with a vague feeling of dissatisfaction at their inability to cope with a 'subject' that they have been led to believe not only exists but also is fundamental to the personal and social development of every child; yet they have found that when they stretch out to grasp it, it separates into a hundred mocking shadows. This makes any final and comprehensive solution to the 'I'd like to do some drama but . . .' problem very difficult, and it is certainly not intended to attempt such a total solution here.

Instead, I propose to take a section of what has recently come to be called 'educational drama' and relate it to the English teacher's concern with language. In the past English and drama have not always been happy bedfellows, with the traditional English teacher suspicious of the exaggerated emphasis upon emotion, and the general sloppiness and lack of discipline that he saw in some drama teaching, while the drama teacher was highly critical of the academic approach to script and the facile 'play-acting' approach to unscripted drama that were perpetrated by some English teachers. This is unfortunate because both have a major common concern—*language*. Recent developments in sociology and linguistics have emphasized very strongly that this concern is not just common to English and drama but fundamental to the educational process as a whole. This common ground can be expressed, albeit in a simplified form, by the following series of propositions:

1 The development of pupils' language is the central concern of the English teacher.
2 Language is developed in situations and especially through social interactions.
3 The commonest, and often most important, uses of language in adult life are in social interactions, normally involving speech.
4 Situations and social interactions involving the use of spoken language form a central part of the subject matter of improvised and scripted drama.[2]

If you accept these propostions, then not only is it true that English and drama have much in common, but also that what they have in common is central to the educational process. It is the nature of this central area and its practical implications for the secondary teacher that form the substance of this book.

If a book of this kind is to do anything of value, however, it has to attempt a fairly detailed solution of the 'I'd like to do some drama but ...' problem. A gloss on the six original sentences will provide criteria that have to be satisfied if this is to be done.

'I'd like to do some drama . . .
1 . . . but I'm worried about discipline.' The approach offered, there-fore, must be able to be applied using the same disciplinary constraints as operate in the English room. When there are problems it must be possible to devise *techniques* for solving them without the teacher having to work under an assumed burden of personal failure.
2 . . . but the headmaster complains if there's too much noise.' It is impossible to talk about drama teaching without a careful consideration of the school context. The work offered must be such that it can be used in an ordinary school with the usual pressures and problems and often without proper facilities.

3 ... but I don't feel confident.' The teacher must feel no more 'at risk' than he does in any other part of his teaching. There must be a *rationale* that he understands (and can, if necessary, explain) and specific techniques he can apply.

4 ... but I haven't got time.' So the rationale must relate the work clearly and uncompromisingly to the central concern of language development.

5 ... but I don't know where to begin' and

6 ... but once I've begun I don't know how to progress.' The rationale that is offered must be broad enough to give a clear over-view of what is involved and detailed enough for lesson-by-lesson application. The techniques must be sufficiently detailed and practical for ready classroom application and backed up with ideas about the generating of teaching material and information about where to find ready-made material.

It will be noticed that in over half of these propositions the word 'rationale' is used. It is essential to provide a clear theoretical background based on recognizable academic disciplines before one can hope to develop useable (and, equally important, educationally justifiable) techniques. This is what many drama specialists have failed to do in the past and their failure is all the more frustrating since the methods that many of them use are not only viable but also of considerable educational importance. The next two chapters, therefore, are largely theoretical, while Chapters 6, 7, and 8 develop techniques from the rationale established in them. The intermediate chapters (Chapters 3, 4, and 5) cover some practical points concerning the school context and work on the improvised situation in general. The final chapters (Chapters 9 and 10) list some available material, and the Bibliography gives details of books referred to in the text and in the notes at the end of each chapter.

## Notes

1 A term used by Peter Doughty (1974) to describe 'an approach to the teaching of English which has developed over the last decade and embraces a loose association of ideas, attitudes, and assumptions about the work of the English teacher which have together radically changed its orientation.'

He distinguishes four features of this consensus:

1 *'Flexibility'* by which what is done in the classroom can be related to the needs of pupils at the time.
2 'A very broad view of the range of concerns which it is possible for the teacher of English to focus upon.'
3 'The idea of the teacher's capacity for *continuous creativity* in the learning situation.'
4 A *change of role* whereby the teacher moves 'from being an *instructor* to being an *entrepreneur* and a *consultant*', and the pupil moves 'from being a passive *recipient* of information to being a *participant* and a *researcher*'.

2  A series of propositions endorsed by the Bullock Committee in *A Language for Life* (H.M.S.O., 1975):

... quite apart from its other qualities it is improvisation, involving the complicated relationships between the written and the spoken word, which seems to us to have particular value for language development.

In the relevant sections of the report (10.31 to 10.42) and in recommendations 120–123 the general concerns of the present book are followed fairly closely.

# 1

# Language, situation, and the individual

## 1.1 Language and situation

My 18-month-old daughter produced the following three utterances the other day:

'boy . . . boy . . . boy'

As they stand, their meaning is obscure. It is slightly clearer if we add intonation patterns and relative volume:

'bóy . . . bòy . . . BOY!'

But this only establishes that the first utterance is a question, the second a statement, and the third emphatic. If we add a description of the relevant features of the situation, however, we can see what she is saying. She was in the centre of the living-room and heard children's voices outside: 'boy?' she asked, and made her way to the french window. From there she could see the children playing: 'boy', she affirmed. Unfortunately, it was time to go upstairs, and so she was picked up and carried away from the window: 'BOY!' she complained. Thus, knowing the situation, we could translate her utterances as:

Is that a boy outside?
There is a boy outside.
Put me down—I want to see the boy!

The example is taken from the speech of a very young child, but it illustrates the general interdependence of situation and language. Halliday (1974b) gives a more complex view of the relationship:

The 'situation' is a theoretical sociolinguistic construct; it is for this reason that we interpret a particular situation type or social context, as a semiotic structure. The semiotic structure of a situation type can be represented as a complex of three dimensions: the ongoing social activity, the role relationships involved, and the symbolic or rhetorical channel. We shall refer to these respectively as *field, tenor* and *mode* . . . . The field . . . is the field of social action in which the text is embedded; it includes the subject matter, as one special manifestation. The tenor . . . is the set of role relationships among the relevant participants; it includes levels of formality as one particular instance. The mode . . . is the channel or wavelength selected, which is essentially the function that is assigned to language in the total structure of the situation . . .

As Halliday implies, the language used in the situation will be conditioned by the needs of the situation. Take, for example, a simple request for help.

If a teacher is speaking to a pupil he might say:
'Harris, would you carry this for me, please?' (1)

If he met the same pupil in the street, he might phrase his request:
'John, you couldn't possibly give me a hand with this, could you?' (2)

If he was talking to his wife in the street, he might say:
'Hullo love, give us a hand with this, will you?' (3)

As the tenor and the field changed, so too did the form of language used.

### 1.1.1 Levels of language

If we wish to define the changes that have taken place, then we must distinguish a number of different levels at which linguistic choices are made. First, the *grammatical forms* used vary from situation to situation. In (1) the teacher says, ' . . . would you carry this for me, please?' but by (3) this has become ' . . . give us a hand with this, will you?' The polite request form, using 'would', has been replaced by the imperative 'give', followed by the softening question, 'will you?' The words used, or *lexis*, have also changed. 'Harris' in (1) becomes 'John' in (2). Similarly, the slightly formal 'carry' gives way to the more relaxed 'give . . . a hand with'. It is not always easy or useful, however, to make a rigid distinction between words and the ways in which we combine, order, and modify them to create sentences. It is more convenient to consider one system, the *lexico-grammatical* system.

The sound system of language, its *phonology*, is also affected when the situation alters. The lexical choices that are made will necessitate an appropriate phonemic selection. (Phonemes are the significant sounds of which language is composed: the smallest sound alterations that one can make to an utterance and still alter its meaning. Thus there is a difference of meaning between the two words that are written as 'pad' and 'bad' because in English /p/ and /b/ are phonemes. Other languages might not distinguish between them.) The grammatical selection in turn implies a particular tone pattern, or a choice from a limited range of possible tone patterns. Sometimes, too, a change in social situation will necessitate a change in accent, which affects the production of individual phonemes. Thus a Yorkshireman selling insurance in Bournemouth may feel socially constrained to suppress his home accent and use the long 'a' sound instead of the short in words like 'path' when he is at work.[1]

### 1.1.2 Paralanguage

Phonology, lexis, and grammar are not, however, the only elements that contribute to communication. By subtle alterations of tone and emphasis we can in fact modify the meaning of the words and structures we use. The same arrangement of words can be made polite, aggressive, tentative, or pleading by changes of tonal quality, timing, stress, and juncture. Such extra-linguistic features are referred to as paralanguage since they convey meaning outside, or parallel to, the linguistic meaning. The extra-linguistic information that can be carried by a social interaction is, however, very much broader than this. 'We speak with our vocal organs but we converse with our whole bodies; conversation consists of much more than a simple interchange of spoken words' (Abercrombie, 1968). In conversation, gesture, facial expression, posture, and relative positioning all provide a gloss on what is being said, and without this information it is difficult to understand what is being said, or even to converse at all.

Any one who doubts this should try the experiment of speaking to someone they don't know very well, while sitting or standing in such a position that they can't see each other. They will find that such a conversation is very difficult to sustain, especially if it is restricted to 'pure' language by the rule that they are not allowed to make any sounds that are not words—no 'er', 'um', 'mmmmm', or 'uh huh'. For a start, it becomes very hard to know whether the other person is paying attention to you or not, or to be sure when they have finished speaking and you should start. As a result, there are many interruptions and false starts. Worse than this, it is exceedingly difficult to work out the attitude of the other person to you and to what you are saying, and to decide whether he is sincere or not in what he is saying.

We judge not only a person's sincerity but also his whole emotional attitude, the impression he is trying to create, by the small signs that are given off during the course of an interaction. A raised eyebrow, a refusal to meet a glance, or a slight movement of the whole body away from the other can all convey as much meaning as several sentences; indeed, it is frequently a meaning that could not be put into sentences. Although people may interpret gestures and expressions in different ways, there is general agreement about the pieces of behaviour on which judgements of another person's intentions may be based. These may be briefly listed as: direction of gaze, facial expression, gesture, posture, and relative positioning. This behaviour is not innate, it is learned--a fact that is witnessed by the way it can vary from culture to culture. Like language, paralanguage can be learned with varying degrees of success. Like language, too, it is learned in situations, and is limited by the range of situations that the learner experiences.[2]

### 1.1.3 Meaning

So far the analysis would appear to be relatively clear cut. According to the social situation in which we find ourselves we select the appropriate linguistic and paralinguistic behaviour. The kind of language chosen in a situation is generally referred to as 'register' and a person's skill (and satisfaction) in dealing with social life is clearly dependent upon a sophisticated control of a range of different linguistic registers. Such an analysis is, however, misleading if it implies that the individual has a kind of mental card-index of communicative behaviour from which he can freely choose within any situation: as though people always can and sometimes do make deliberately wrong choices. As Halliday (1974b) points out, such a definition of register omits the most important feature which governs all the rest, meaning:

A register can be defined as the configuration of semantic resources that the member of a culture typically associates with a situation type. It is the meaning potential that is accessible in a given social context . . . the register is recognizable as a particular selection of words and structures. But it is defined in terms of meanings.[3]

We learn our mother tongue in specific situations and therefore we not only associate certain types of vocabulary, grammar, and vocal production with specific situations, but we can only associate certain meaning possibilities with them as well.

We thus have a 'three-decker' model of language:

the semantic level
the lexico-grammatical level
the phonological (or orthographic) level.

In addition we are aware that communicative behaviour within a situation is not confined to language but may include a wide range of paralinguistic elements as well. The educational relevance of all this can perhaps best be seen by observing what happens when things go wrong.

### 1.1.4 The language of failure

A striking example of how language fails occurred in a TV programme based on the B.B.C. series 'The Family'. a TV camera and sound crew lived with a 'typical' working-class family over a period of weeks, recording the events of their everyday lives. After the series had ended, a retrospective programme was screened in which one or two key incidents were followed through several programmes and then analysed by a psychologist and a sociologist. One major incident concerned the difficulties that a young working-class couple were having in getting a council house. Three main sequences from the original programme were shown.

In the first scene the young couple were writing a letter to the local housing department. The wife was actually writing it, while her husband read a magazine and offered advice, suggesting suitable phrases and sometimes whole sentences. The letter dwelt on the inconvenience and distress that was being caused to the mother and small baby because the family had to live in one room at her mother-in-law's house. The general tenor of the letter was thus pleading and personal. Husband and wife were both very concerned that all the words used (and the husband appeared to have quite a wide vocabulary) were spelled correctly.

In the second scene the wife had received a rather unhelpful letter from the housing department which she discussed with her mother-in-law. The mother-in-law told her that she must go to the council offices and keep on going there until they got fed up with her. She should take the letter and be angry with the official who had written it. She should tell him that they had been told (that is, by the mother-in-law) that they had a month in which to find somewhere else to live. The daughter-in-law said that she could not be angry just like that, so the mother-in-law offered to hit her just before she went out, in order to get her into the right mood.

In the third scene the daughter-in-law did eventually meet an official of the housing department. She was not angry but she did explain what her mother-in-law had said about finding somewhere else to live. The official listened politely and then told the daughter-in-law that when she had a firm eviction date she would be allocated to a council hostel! The girl was left looking as though some kind of trick had been performed but she was not sure how or what.

The failure of the young couple was essentially a failure of language. To begin with they had difficulty with the sheer mechanics of producing written language (spelling and writing a letter), and with the mechanics of producing spoken language (the 'acceptable' pronunciation of some words). These, however, were minor problems. Much more serious was their inability to use the vocabulary and grammar of language in ways that were appropriate to their needs. In the letter the daughter-in-law wrote, she used grammatical forms that may have been correct, and employed words in ways that a dictionary might justify, but the final product was not a letter that would achieve her ends. She dwelt on the emotional aspects of the situation in such a way that the letter became a personal plea for help. The official who received it would probably be quite accustomed to dealing with such letters, and would not be in a position to respond at that personal level even if that were desirable. All the letter did was to trigger off a stock official response, an outcome that could have been predicted even before the letter was posted.

The preparation for the interview with the housing official and the interview itself displayed a similar confusion about using language. The daughter-in-law could not use language forms other than the rather personal ones she was accustomed to using within the family, nor was her mother-in-law able to help her. The suggestion that the mother-in-law should strike her daughter-in-law just before she left for the council offices typified this confusion between the kind of emotional expression appropriate within a family and the indignation that was most likely to be effective when dealing with a cautious, smug, or obstructive local government officer. Since the official was secure in her own role and 'protected' by all the paraphernalia of office, telephones, secretaries, and so on, it is not surprising that the wife's uncertainty about how to behave in such a situation led to failure. She had not, in sociological terms, differentiated between her role as mother and her role as 'ratepayer with a grievance', and so she could not select the right form of language—vocabulary, grammar, and pronunciation—for the situation.

This would have been bad enough, but her language failure went deeper. Or rather, her language failure was because of a deeper failure. It isn't just a question of selecting the right behaviour for a particular situation in one's life, of saying to oneself 'Ah yes, interview with housing officer, so I should adopt role A and use vocabulary B, syntax C, and so on'. People clearly don't live their lives like that. They certainly behave in different ways in different situations, but the choices they make are at an intuitive level and based on the way in which they intuitively interpret a situation. From our experience of social life we learn a series of interpretations, or meanings, to put on the situations in which we find ourselves and as a result we behave in ways that experience has shown to be appropriate. When neither we nor the cultural group to which we belong have specific experience of a particular type of situation, then we tend to equate it to a situation that we do know. Thus we may lump together a range of situations that others will find it necessary or useful to differentiate. The young mother coped well with the traditional roles of mother, wife, and housekeeper, but when she was faced with problems beyond this immediate family context she had to fall back on an 'Us and Them' interpretation of life, which groups together Council Officials, Store Managers, Employers, Politicians, Headmasters, and any others with whom people have to deal or by whom they are affected but whom they may misunderstand, mistrust, or feel threatened by. If one can only interpret such situations in 'Us and Them' terms, then one is not equipped for success. Success requires the ability to differentiate situations adequately before we can hope to frame an appropriate course of action. This is not just a question of knowledge; it is the result of the ways in which we have experienced the use of language in childhood and adolescence, especially within the family.[4]

## 1.2 Language and the individual

### 1.2.1 Roles

The ways in which the resources of the language are deployed by the individual is partly dependent upon the social role that is assumed in a particular situation. In the example quoted in 1.1, one of the reasons why the teacher used different registers in (1) and in (3) was because his role had changed from 'teacher' to 'husband'. Part of the process of growing up is concerned with learning to distinguish and then to play such different roles in different situations, and with acquiring the linguistic resources to go with these roles. Early on the child learns that the teacher is not Mummy and that behaviour which is welcomed at home may be criticized or even mocked at school. The teenager learns that the role of fellow-pupil at school may not be the same as gang-comrade on the street, even if the same individuals are involved, and that the wrong choice may lead to ridicule and embarrassment.

Learning to perceive and identify different situations, to assume the correct role and to manipulate language accordingly, is fundamental to the process of socialization that takes place at home and at school in childhood and adolescence. We have to 'learn' the major roles we shall have to play in adult life, particularly those concerned with family and work, as well as acquiring sufficient skill in 'ad-libbing' to cover those situations for which we have not been specifically prepared by upbringing and formal education. (In everyday life, as Goffman, 1959, points out, the individual has to 'learn enough pieces of expression to be able to "fill in" and manage more or less any part that he is likely to be given.') What happens when this process is left incomplete has already been shown in the incidents quoted from 'The Family'. The fact that the daughter was unable to differentiate adequately between her role as mother and her role as client-with-a-justified-grievance contributed to her failure to communicate with the official. Improvised drama offers opportunities both for experimenting with different social roles and role-relationships, and for analysing them in terms of the physical and linguistic behaviour they produce.

### 1.2.2 The real me

Although people tacitly accept that they play different roles in different situations, they also assume that they have a consistent self; I take it for granted that, underneath all the various ways that I behave in different situations, there is a 'real me'. When we consider language and the individual, we are concerned not only with utterances in social situations, but also with 'what goes on inside your head'. I may speak and act very differently at various times of the day, but my interior language is busily at work relating one 'scene' to another and all of them to my whole past. Thus I have personal continuity 'between' situations.

An approach to drama and language that only took the fragmentary or analytical view that has been detailed so far would not satisfy either personal experience or the broader claim that education, and particularly education in English and drama, is concerned with the whole person. This concern is particularly important when we consider that secondary schooling coincides with that period of human development during which

there is increasing pressure to develop a unified identity which represents basic values and permanent commitments . . . the growth spurt and the development of sexual maturity are probably responsible for the changes in identity; the body image is changed and this creates a heightened concern with the reactions of others. At the same time . . . the adolescent now has a strong desire to break away from a dependent relationship with parents and wants to establish himself or herself as an independent person on equal terms with adults. The pressures to achieve a unified identity are of two main kinds. (1) During adolescence a number of important, and relatively final, decisions have to be made . . . (for example, 'vocation', 'political and religious attitudes') . . . . (2) there is a striving for consistency within the personality. (Argyle, 1969)

### 1.2.3 Language and personality

How the individual's 'interior language' operates to provide a link between this search for personal consistency and the shifting experience of role and situation is explained by Halliday (1974a):

Let us start with the notion of the individual human organism, the human being as a biological specimen. Like the individual in many other species, he is destined to become one of a group, but unlike those of all other species, he achieves this—not wholly, but critically—through language. It is by means of language that the 'human being' becomes one of a group of 'people'. But 'people' in turn, consist of 'persons'; by virtue of his participation in a group the individual is no longer simply a biological specimen of humanity—he is a person. Again language is the essential element in the process, since it is largely the linguistic interchange with the group that determines the status of the individuals and shapes them as persons. The picture is:

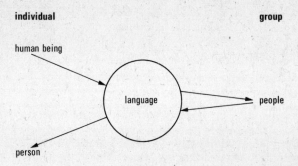

*Figure* 1

In other words, instead of looking at the group as a derivation from and extension of the biologically endowed mental powers of the individual, we explain the nature of the individual as a derivation from and extension of his participation in the group . . . .

But when we do adopt this perspective it becomes apparent that we can take the dialectic one stage farther and that when we do so, language will still remain the crucial factor. The individual as a 'person' is now a potential 'member': he has the capacity to function within society, and once more it is through language that he achieves this status. How does a society differ from a group as we conceive it here? A group is a simple structure, a set of participants among whom there are no special relations, only the simple coexistence that is implied by participation in the group. A society, on the other hand, does not consist of participants but of relations, and these relations define social roles. Being a member of society means occupying a social role; and it is again by means of language that a 'person' becomes potentially the occupant of a social role.

Social roles are combinable, and the individual, as a member of a society, occupies not just one role but many at a time, always through the medium of language. Language is again a necessary condition for this final element in the process of the development of the individual, from human being to person to what we may call 'personality', a personality being interpreted as a role complex. Here the individual is seen as the configuration of a number of roles defined by the social relationships in which he enters; from these roles he synthesizes a personality. Our model now looks like this:

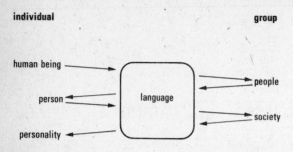

*Figure* 2

Let us know interpret this in terms of a perspective on language. We have gone a long way round in order to reach this particular angle of vision, certainly over-simplifying the picture and perhaps seeming to exaggerate the importance of language in the total process. The justification for this is that we have been trying to achieve a perspective that will be most relevant in an educational context. From this point of view, language is the medium through which a human being becomes a personality, in consequence of his membership of society and his occupancy of social roles. The concept of language as behaviour, as a form of interaction between man and man, is turned round, as it were, so that it throws light on the individual: the formation of the personality is itself a social process, or a complex of social processes, and language—by virtue of is social function—plays the key part in it.

## 1.3 Summary

We may consider language as a semantic system, a lexico-grammatical system, or a phonological system, but at whichever level we study language we cannot separate it from the situations in which it occurs. The significant features of the situation—field, tenor, and mode—will determine the register that is employed, as well as affecting the paralinguistic features that occur. Situation is thus of fundamental importance whether our approach to language is one of analysis or of synthesis. If it is one of analysis, then we shall be concerned to see how meaning, grammar, lexis, and phonology are affected by situation and how the individual human being alters his linguistic and paralinguistic behaviour according to the various social and linguistic roles he is called upon to play. The synthesizing approach, on the other hand, leads to an examination of how situations combine to make up a life, and roles combine to make up a personality. The practical applications of such analysis and synthesis are the subject matter of Chapters 6 and 7 respectively.

## Notes

1 Strictly speaking this is a dialect difference, dialect being defined as 'variety of language according to user' (Halliday *et al*. 1964), whereas here we are more concerned with variety of language according to use. However, since people can and do alter their dialect according to social requirements, the example is relevant here.

2 It has become customary to break down into further technical subdivisions the behaviour I have lumped together as 'extra-linguistic'. The usual subdivision is as follows: *paralanguage* (vocal effects); *kinesics* (physical movement, that is, gesture, facial expression, and so on); *proxemics* (relative positioning, use of physical properties, such as tables, chairs, a manager's desk, and so on). This subdivision is not particularly useful for the present purposes, however, so the term 'paralanguage' will generally be used to cover all such types of behaviour.

3 See also Halliday (1974a).

4 Professor Bernstein and his team at the London Institute of Education have developed a series of theories and research projects in this area (Bernstein, 1971 and 1972). A short summary of what this means in terms of language is given by Halliday (1974a) who writes:

All human beings put language to certain types of use, and all of them learn a linguistic system which has evolved in that context, but what aspects of the system are typically deployed and emphasized in one type of use or another is to a significant extent determined by the culture—by the systems of social relations in which the child grows up, including the roles he himself learns to recognize and to adopt. All children have access to the meaning potential of the system, but they may differ, because social groups differ, in their interpretation of what the situation demands.

17

# 2
# Imitation

The consideration of language in the previous chapter indicated that it was highly desirable to use imaginary situations in order to extend our pupils' experience of language. What makes such an extension possible is the propensity human beings have to imitate. Imitative play occurs at all stages of human development, from very early childhood to old age, but obviously its uses for the individual and its general functions in human development vary considerably from stage to stage.

## 2.1 The exploratory model

The commonest model of imitative behaviour that is used to justify educational drama is that of the exploratory dramatic play of childhood. An example will make this clear. Let us imagine a group of three children of, say, 9 or 10. One is hiding behind a low wall holding a stick as if it were a gun. Two others approach warily, not quite sure where he is. When they are almost up to him he leaps out at them and subjects them to a withering burst of machine-gun fire. One of them dies spectacularly and lies still, groaning slightly, but the other runs away, ducking and weaving as he runs.
'You're dead!' shouts the attacker.
'No—you missed,' replies the fleeing child, and he stops to aim a single pistol shot at the attacker, who now takes up the chase. The dead man lies still.

The movement and speech of the children are characterized by a number of qualities that have been observed by many writers on the subject: they are *absorbed* in what they are doing and their 'acting' shows all the *sincerity* of which they are capable; their movements are often graceful and agile; they are *unaware of any audience* their playing may accidentally have. At the moment of playing, their imaginative experience is to them as real as—indeed, if not more real than—'real' life.

## Imitation

It is this type of imitative play that most writers about educational drama have taken as the starting point for work in school.[1] Its function in human development is clearly important. It helps to develop physical and verbal skills; children can master experiences and emotions that would otherwise cause serious problems (for example, the fear of death in the play just described); the child can make any experience 'part of himself' by physically 'doing it'; and, through playing the roles of adult life, children prepare for what is to happen to them later. Pemberton-Billing and Clegg (1965) argue that the school can use this process and develop it further than it might naturally go:

Through this play the child learns to grow up. He comes to grips gradually with the real world . . . . The drama teacher's job is to discipline and direct the child's play into channels where he needs to make worthwhile decisions and discoveries.

There is no doubt that this 'exploratory' model of imitative behaviour is very useful for school drama. If we can attain the right working conditions, in which the qualities of absorption, sincerity, and unawareness of audience can be achieved, then we can use this type of imitative play as a means of exploring new experiences, and of coming to terms with feelings and thoughts that may otherwise be disturbing. We can also compensate for the narrowness and restrictions of the real world that many of our children live in, by providing a wealth of imaginative experience that will broaden their mental horizons. Linguistically this is important: the resources of language are available to all, but the ways in which they are actually put to use will be determined by the culture in which a child is brought up, 'by the system of social relations in which the child grows up, including the roles he himself learns to recognize and adopt' (Halliday, 1974a). Whatever the home culture may be, the school can attempt to extend it linguistically by providing imaginary situations that offer the child roles, relationships, and problems that go beyond his daily experience and make demands upon him that he has not had to face before.

The exploratory model has its limitations, however. It has already been pointed out that a prerequisite for success is that the work be characterized by 'absorption', 'sincerity', and 'unawareness of audience'. Anyone who has tried introducing drama to a third year secondary class will know just what problems that involves. Most 13-year-olds are only too aware of everyone else in classroom or studio and in many cases it is well nigh impossible to achieve absorption and the consequent

sincerity and 'reality' of experience. The original example of this type
of imitative behaviour was taken from the play of younger children;
indeed most of the observations of human behaviour upon which the
*conventional* theory of educational drama is based are of pre-adolescent
behaviour.[2] By the end of the first year of secondary education this
kind of play has largely disappeared (possibly hastened by the transfer
from primary schools). Reasons for prolonging it artificially are hard to
find, and the onset of puberty brings with it problems that are likely to
militate against work based on exploratory imitation.

As a result of the difficulty many adolescents have in overcoming
their awareness of others and in being absorbed in their activity, some
drama teachers following the exploratory model begin to pursue involvement for its own sake. The darkened studio, coloured lights, and powerful rhythmic music that they often employ combine to produce a
working atmosphere that verges on the hypnotic. Increasingly, any contribution that does not carry a high emotional charge is undervalued.
Such an approach is not only absurd, it may be dangerous. In any case,
it mistakes the means for the end. The original observation was that
absorption (a milder and more sympathetic term than 'involvement')
tended to be present in that kind of play where children dealt with
those aspects of experience that were difficult, strange, or merely new.
As a result the imaginary situation appeared to them at the time to be
'real' and thus became a part of their total mental experience. If such
absorption is difficult, particularly with adolescents, and in the early
stages of work in drama, this is not a criticism of the teacher or of the
learner, but rather a comment on what is involved in growing up in our
society.[3]

## 2.2 The illustrative model

If we look at the way in which adolescents use imitation, then we get a
rather different picture, and, as a result, a somewhat altered model. A
group of 12-year olds is talking to a teacher about the attitudes of adults.
They come to the conclusion that in general adults are very strict. When
asked by the teacher what they mean by 'strict', the children give
various examples:

MARK Some old people me and John met at the bus stop, we pushed
in front of them. You know, because the bus was there, we went in the

bus and they got on with us and pulled us back . . . . (*He adopts a grumbling, high-pitched voice.*) 'Mmmmmmmmer . . . mmmmmmermmm . . . mmmmmmmer . . . .' They was talking like that.

IAN  Like me mum. Every time—I can't do nothing right in that place. I get a bit of bread and butter to eat. (*He raises his voice in imitation of an adult shouting across a room.*) 'What you get that for? Tea's in a minute!' (*The rest of the class laughs, so he embroiders.*) 'Get the coal!'*[4]

Here the behaviour of the adolescents is characterized by qualities that are very different from those to be seen in the imitative activities of the younger children described above. The speakers are very *aware of their audience* and imitation is no longer an end in itself. Instead their imitative behaviour is used to help them *communicate* with others in a social interaction. They imitate other people's behaviour in order to back up some analytical point they wish to make: this type of person behaves in this way, they say, and here's an example to prove it.

Adolescents are very interested in the ways in which people behave and in the reasons for different forms of behaviour. Argyle (1969) explains why, in a discussion of the nature of adolescent groups:

Conversation is mainly about other adolescents, parents, interpersonal feelings and social interaction. These are probably the only natural groups that discuss social interaction. Such topics are discussed because adolescents have problems to solve in this area—as well as working out an identity and establishing a changed relationship with adults, they have to acquire the social skills of dealing with the opposite sex, to come to terms with the difficulty of playing different roles on different occasions, and having relationships of different degrees of intimacy with different people.

In such conversation the imitation of linguistic and/or paralinguistic behaviour is used as a form of illustration. It may stay at the level of simple verbal copying, or take the more elaborate form of a full-scale acted impersonation; it will serve to prove a point, to stimulate discussion about ways of behaving in social interactions, or to enlighten the speaker's audience in some other way. For classroom purposes, this type of imitation is clearly easier to use and indeed it may come naturally into classroom discussion, as the conversation between Mark and Ian did. It is only a short step from this to getting a class to improvise the whole situation and then dicussing with them the kind of behaviour it involved.

Underlying our behaviour in social situations there is a wide range of assumptions upon which we base our conduct. These cover not only matters of appropriateness of language, and of social role, but things like how we interpret the posture and facial expressions of a person we are talking to. These judgements, which in the broadest sense might be said to form part of Doughty's 'folk linguistic',[5] are based on experience. Thus, while assumptions may be shared by a large number of people, different groups inevitably have different assumptions. An important part of growing up is learning to relate our own private 'interpretative criteria' to those of the other people in our culture. When an imaginary situation is set up in which the emphasis is upon some aspect of social behaviour, opportunities are provided both in the improvisation itself and in the following discussion for the participants to make explicit the assumptions that underlie their behaviour in such situations and that normally remain implicit.

## 2.3 The expressive model

There remains a third model of imitative behaviour that is relevant to classroom drama. This is similar to the illustrative model, but differs from it in several important respects. It is best exemplified by the German playwright and poet Bertolt Brecht (1939):

. . . an incident such as can be seen at any street corner: an eyewitness demonstrating to a collection of people how a traffic accident took place. The bystanders may not have observed what happened, or they may simply not agree with him, may 'see things in a different way'; the point is that the demonstrator acts the behaviour of a driver or victim or both in such a way that the bystanders are able to form an opinion about the accident . . . . The demonstration should have a socially practical significance. Whether our street demonstrator is out to show that one attitude on the part of the driver or pedestrian makes an accident inevitable where another would not, or whether he is demonstrating with a view to fixing the responsibility, his demonstration has a practical purpose, intervenes socially.

The emphasis is once again upon communication, but the circumstances and the setting alter the form of the communication. It is far more public, for the speaker may well not know his audience, and the subject-matter is broader and more complex. Rather than analysing aspects of behaviour in interpersonal relationships, the speaker is concerned to communicate both factual information about an event and comment on its general social significance. This is close to the expressive form of adult theatre, but, as Brecht makes clear, it is a form of theatre in which *what* is communicated is important both to actors and audience.

This type of imitative behaviour is rather less common than the other two. Relatively few people have the desire or the confidence to set up the kind of 'one-man performance' described by Brecht. But it is surprising how consistently children demand to 'do a play', or to perform work in front of an audience. I say 'surprising' because it has become almost a cliche of drama teaching books that a clear distinction should be made between drama and theatre, and that any thought of performance should be ruled out until a fairly late stage. If this is right, then why do so many children, in any class, want to engage in theatre, on however small a scale? They may, of course, be conditioned to: after all, when headmasters and others tend to think of drama as meaning only the production and presentation of plays, children are likely to pick up the same ideas. More important, however, is the fairly natural desire people have when they have been working on a project, particularly one involving group effort, to share it with others. Behind all this, however, is the consistent need to communicate.

Theatrical communication is very different from other forms of communication open to young people. In schools there is still massive emphasis on written language, and only recently some belated recognition of oracy. But theatrical communication is different from people just talking to each other and from written communications such as the essay, the novel, or poetry: it involves a structured combination of visual and auditory elements, and it exists in time. There is no 'turning back a few pages' with a play, or with television; all one can do is depend on one's memory of the impression, and this is constantly being affected, altered, and updated by fresh aural and visual sensations. Theatrical communication is also more likely than other forms of communication to be non-literal and non-linear. Acting is non-literal because it involves impersonation, and, like the novel, the theatrical message is selective in its presentation. The play presents us with a 'message' that we can perceive as 'true' using means that are decidedly contrived and fictional. (Strangely, often the more contrived the means, the greater the force with which the truth can strike.) The audio-visual aspect of the play also increases the possibilities of non-linear communication— communication in which an impression is created through the juxtaposition of items, words, or ideas, rather than through logical development.

Different means of communication open up new dimensions in what is communicated, and for this reason alone theatrical communication is valuable to our pupils. However, the importance of TV in our lives is another, vital reason for understanding the limits and effects of this type of communication. Much of our pupils' leisure time is heavily influenced by TV and much of what is actually shown on TV is directly influenced by the nature of the medium. The news broadcast, for example, which we used to think of as a 'linear' presentation of facts (admittedly selected), has now become a non-linear and non-literal presentation, in which link-men, reporters, experts, and interviewers play parts, express emotions, take on provocative roles in staged confrontations, as if the news were being 'created' before our very eyes. Children's own work on theatrical communication can help them towards a general understanding of these influences, and, perhaps, begin the slow process of correcting the imbalance between the professional 'communicators' and their audience.

It is, however, worth pointing out that this third model is not without its problems when we come to apply it in the secondary school. Brecht's example indicated that the theatrical message originates in the experience of the actor/storyteller and that its function is at least partly persuasive. In the school, therefore, this would mean pupils talking to pupils in language that they understand about subjects that they think are important. Normally the school and its teachers exercise an easy but powerful control over both the situation[6] and the language that is used within it, as Creber (1972) points out in an imaginary dialogue:

BOY When I was . . .
TEACHER Say SIR when you speak to a member of staff.
BOY Sir, . . . I was at . . .
TEACHER And take your hands out of your pockets. I don't speak to the Headmaster with my hands in my pockets . . .
BOY Sorry—
TEACHER . . . or leaning on a radiator
BOY Sorry—sorry, SIR . . . when I was at Blacton . . .
TEACHER Well boy, get on with it—when you were at Blacton . . . ?
BOY Yes, sir, when I was at Blacton Primary School . . . we used to go bird-watching on the cliffs and . . .
TEACHER Jones, I suppose you know what this lesson is . . . ?

Although this is a parody of what Creber says 'is now largely confined in state schools to teachers with minor personality disorders', he points out that 'kids are still often dominated, perhaps more subtly, by the teacher's language'. The revolutionary nature of a truly pupil-centred theatre is that it would cede control of the situation and of the language in which it was expressed to the children. This form of theatre is obviously a long way from the school play, and just how effective it is will depend on the circumstances of the school involved. Because of theatrical convention, there would be no chance for teachers to interrupt and redefine the situation or to attempt to control the way in which it was languaged, without totally destroying it as an act of theatre. This is a set of conditions that many teachers, and especially headmasters, are not prepared to face.[7]

## 2.4 Conclusion: using the imaginary situation

Although three models of imitative behaviour have now been outlined, for classroom purposes the first two—the exploratory and the illustrative—really need to be considered together. Growth into adolescence sees a natural move away from the absorbed, sincere type of imitative play that characterizes childhood towards a more conscious, even 'calculating' use of it for illustrative purposes in social interactions. The easiest and most obvious way to begin using imitative behaviour in the classroom with adolescents is to set up an imaginary situation in which the students are mainly required to make some kind of comment on human social behaviour. (To use the terms introduced in Chapter 1, the work will be mainly analytical at first.) Initially such comment may seem very superficial to the teacher, but he must make allowance for the novelty of the activity (in school at least) and not in any case attempt to impose his own adult judgement in the early stages.

As the work progresses, however, it will be found with many classes that the qualities of absorption and sincerity that typify the exploratory model begin to appear in improvisations. Often this growth will be very uneven, so that the depth of experience gained in any one lesson will vary greatly from pupil to pupil. While some will be deeply involved in an improvisation, others will find that they remain largely outside the situation, watching their own interpretation of role and relationship. Thus, when the working method has been established, the students will be able to, and want to, set situations into some kind of broader social context, and so synthesis will begin to complement the analytical work already done. This combination of improvisation with group and class discussion, working on both analysis and synthesis, is described in detail in Chapters 6 and 7.

There remains the expressive model, which is somewhat detached from the other two because it necessitates a different organization of class and lesson. It will often be found that the expressive use of improvised situations will follow the others. It is usually after a certain amount of material of one type has been worked through, and when a class feels confident in handling the material, that the desire to shape it into a piece of theatrical communication is likely to arise. The performance will normally take place first inside the class itself where there is a large amount of shared experience and where the performers are most confident about the communicative relationship between themselves and their audience. Questions about theatrical communication within classes, and with larger groups, are considered in Chapter 8.

## Notes

1  The earliest, and in many ways most representative, examination of this type of play and its relation to educational drama is that of Peter Slade (1954). His work is, however, mainly useful when one is considering children of primary school age and much of what he says, especially about adolescents, looks dated (and even sentimental) from the viewpoint of the mid-1970s.

2  By 'conventional' I mean the tradition of writing about drama exemplified by Slade (1954) and Way (1967).

3  The general inadequacies of this 'exploratory' model are discussed more fully by the author in two articles under the general title of 'The Language of Improvisation' (Seely, 1971a and b).

4  All items marked with an asterisk are quoted verbatim from tape-recordings of actual lessons.

5  A term used by Doughty *et al.* (1972), and explained as follows:

There is a commonsense view of the world that we live in which is sometimes referred to as a 'folk-wisdom' . . . . Our native speaker's intuitions about language and how men use it can thus be referred to as a 'folk linguistic', a 'common sense' about the language we live by.

6 Many teachers have learned that it pays to spare themselves no unpleasantness in order to establish and make secure their dominance in the first few days and weeks of school. They exert themselves particularly to define the situation as one in which the teacher is dominant. Until this definition of the situation is accepted, there will be some conflict . . . .

After the first few weeks in which conflict over the definition has been severe, the hostility toward the teacher dies down; this is in most cases owing to the operation of two factors: use and acceptance of the situation makes the teacher domination bearable to the students, and the teacher relaxes his grip slightly, just enough to give friendly attitudes a chance to spring up within the situation. But these friendly attitudes must always spring up within the situation as defined in terms of teacher domination; if they spring up outside it, they conflict with it, and operate to overthrow the so painfully established social order. (Waller, 1961)

7 These conditions also, I suspect, account for the suspicion with which some headmasters regard even the annual school play. I have, for example, experienced fierce opposition to plays as apparently innocent as *The Dream of Peter Mann* by Bernard Kops and *Johnny Salter* by Aidan Chambers. As far as I can see, both of these are exceedingly moral tales, but in the first case I was told, 'I don't think you should do this', and then, later, 'All right, but it's your responsibility if there's any trouble with parents or governors.' In the second I was informed, amazingly, that it was an 'immoral' play, written by someone who had 'no sensitivity towards children'. When I pointed out that the play had been written by a member of a religious order, the reply came back: 'I thought it had a touch of the Catholic about it'!

# 3

# Practical preliminaries

## 3.1 The school setting

In an ideal world we would now proceed to develop the models described in the last chapter in practical terms. But the world and particularly the schools it contains are far from ideal. Whatever techniques are devised to develop improvisation and the use of imaginary situations must take account of the immediate social and physical settings in which they take place.

The methods of the drama teacher are still, unfortunately, regarded with some suspicion in many of our secondary schools. This is partly historical in origin, partly the result of extravagant claims combined with inept teaching by some practitioners, and partly a result of the nature of the activity itself. It is the last of these that is likely to cause most problems to the practising teacher today.

Some schools depend for what they term 'discipline' upon the establishment of behavioural norms which cannot be questioned and by which the teacher's behaviour is regarded as different in kind from the children's. As one teacher put it: 'If you can't tell a child to get off the grass while you're walking on the grass, then you'll never make a good teacher.' Thus teachers may comment upon, control and even mimic a child's behaviour, but for a child to do any of these things publicly would be considered insolent and a breach of discipline. Illogical though it may seem, there is clearly a strong link in many schools between 'discipline' and the personal immunity assumed by the teacher. But improvisation, which encourages children to observe, simulate, and discuss human behaviour, depends on human models, and, do what we may, the most accessible adult models for our pupils are their teachers. 'If I can do a scene about my father losing his temper, why can't I do one about the headmaster?' seems a perfectly reasonable question, but none the easier to answer for all that. The close attention paid in drama to the noises people make, the words and sentences they use, and the meanings they express is also bound to make our pupils observe those around them—teachers and pupils alike—with greater care, and this attention will not be welcome in all schools.

The traditional concept of 'discipline' also comprehends a fairly narrow range of types of class organization. Some secondary heads, even now, attempt to discourage group work in English, for example, because they believe that it enourages too much talking and consequent indiscipline. Although they may not be aware of it, they still have before them the model of the traditional classroom with its desks in rows and the teacher's high desk placed on a dais at the front. They like to have glass panels let into the classroom doors so that they can prowl along the corridor, peering into each classroom to make sure that 'they've all got their heads down'. They want to see written work coming out of every possible lesson, because they still believe that work equals quiet plus writing. Since drama does not generally involve much in the way of writing and necessitates a lot of noise, the traditionalist view tends to be that not much work is going on either (and if no 'work' is happening, then nothing useful is being learned). Such a school atmosphere has two important effects on the teacher of drama. At the personal level it may mean that he is open to criticism from senior teachers. At the classroom level it can mean that children come to his lessons with attitudes conditioned by what goes on in the rest of the school. If that is 'work', then this is 'play' and not to be taken very seriously. As a result the teacher can be put in a position where he feels that undertaking a drama lesson is just putting his head on the block.

Now it may be felt that this is an excessively gloomy view of the situation and it is true that there is an increasing number of schools where things are much better. At the worst, however, the teacher may find himself in a situation not unlike that described and it is therefore as well to consider whether anything can be done about it. The answer to this may well be 'no'. There are schools where the relationship between pupils and staff is so bad that it is next to impossible to develop the atmosphere of mutual respect, if not trust, in which useful work can be done. Such situations are far less common, however, than those where the teacher experiences difficulties and needs to find ways of overcoming them. At the personal level there is little that can be done beyond establishing with the school hierarchy that drama is part of the curriculum; that in classroom organization it has more in common with the P.E. lesson than an old-fashioned English lesson; and that its legitimate noise level may be expected to be nearer that of music than of maths. If these points are not accepted by the headmaster, at least in principle, it is difficult to see how one can begin. That is not the major problem, however. Where real difficulties tend to be experienced is in the relationship between the teacher and the class. If the class come to a lesson with the assumption that it is not really 'work', then the lesson stands little chance of being successful. This means that the attitudes towards language that are implicit in improvised drama must be those that inform the general teaching of English in the school, and vice versa. You cannot spend four English lessons a week 'gerund grinding' and seriously expect to get useful improvised drama out of the fifth. However, just as there are perfectly disciplined ways of organizing work in the 'new English', so improvisation has its own, but strict, discipline. Provided that this is clearly understood, then there is no reason why children should bring to drama lessons attitudes that are any more unhelpful than those they take to any other lesson.

## 3.2 Concentration

### 3.2.1 Feeling exposed

The kind of problem that is more likely to be encountered, however, is not of the order implied above—a direct threat to the lesson as a whole. It is much more likely to take the form of the example that follows. This comes from a lesson with a mixed class of 11-year-olds in a streamed school (average reading age of class 9½). The class had no previous experience of drama at school.

TEACHER (*to David*). Now, you're an old man, right? And you're waiting at a bus stop: an old man waiting for the bus.
(*To John*). Now John, you're you.
JOHN  Yeah.
TEACHER  You're you, which is quite a part. (*General laughter from class.*) And it's the last bus which is just going to go. And you've got to catch it to go home. And you suddenly discover that you've lost your money. There's nobody around except him—
MARY  The old man!
TEACHER  The old man. You don't know him. You've never seen him

before in your life. (*Pause.*) That's the scene I want you to do, OK?
Now the rest of you very quiet. Right, try that scene—off you go.
(*There is a pause. David and John just stand there. The class start to
giggle. David and John start to giggle. Nothing happens. There are cries
from the class to 'Come on!'*)

TEACHER Ssshh! Quiet now.

JOHN Hullo. I've lost all me money.

(*Another long pause. More giggling. The class begins to grow restless
and fidget and cough.*)

DAVID Hullo. A bit cold, i'n't it?

JOHN (*after pause*). I dunno.

DAVID Whereabouts did you lose it?

JOHN Dunno. I dunno where it is.

DAVID How far away is it then?

JOHN About a hundred yards.

(*Another long pause, more giggling.*)

TEACHER All right, OK.

(*The boys are asked to sit down, then the following conversation takes
place.*)

TEACHER John, is that the best you can do, do you think?

JOHN No, not really.

TEACHER Well, why isn't it the best you can do?

JOHN He kept on making me laugh. I could do it much better without
him.

TEACHER You'd find it difficult to do on your own, wouldn't you?
(*To class generally.*) Why do you think he kept on laughing?

DAVID Because it was funny.

TEACHER Was it meant to be funny?

JOHN No, I just felt funny when there was all the other people looking
at me.*

Superficially, this part of the lesson is a failure and the children are
aware that it is a failure: nothing that approaches anyone's definition
of drama has taken place. What was it that prevented the children from
working effectively?

In the discussion with the teacher, John said two important things.
At the very end, he said:
'I just felt funny when there was all the other people looking at me.'

In other words, a major cause of his unease, and hence laughter, was his awareness of the audience, leading to personal embarrassment. This is such a common experience that it hardly seems worth saying. In the early stages of drama work an audience is nearly always destructive of worthwhile work and sometimes of any work at all. So, we may conclude, the teacher was wrong to make David and John perform the scene in front of the others. He should have devised some method of working which did not involve performance before an audience.

However, John said something else which was also revealing. Earlier he said:

'He (David) kept on making me laugh.'

David, too, was watching him, and this also made him feel embarrassed. Now David was not 'audience' in the normal sense, since he was a participant in the scene, but in early work this often appears to make little difference. John was aware that David was watching him and vice versa. Both felt embarrassed and so the giggling began. Even when the teacher gets the whole class working on solo movement he may still find that there is considerable awareness of the others in the room. The problem is not just a question of 'audience' and 'performance' but of the degree of *exposure* that individual members of a class feel that they are being subjected to.

However, the lesson quoted above was not a complete failure, as it led the class to a realization that there was a problem and to some formulation of what the problem was. Children need to accept that they may feel embarrassed from time to time and that, if they do, it is generally because of their awareness of others. Moreover, they need to be prepared to admit that when they giggle, send the situation up, or otherwise avoid doing what the teacher really wants them to, it is more often than not because of this feeling of being exposed.

This all needs saying because in some writing and teaching about educational drama there has been an unwillingness to face up to the problems implied.[1] Emphasis has been placed upon the positive values of 'involvement' or 'absorption', by which is usually meant a state of mind in which the child is 'wrapped up' in the imaginative activity to the exclusion of all else (see also 2.1). While this emphasis is good, and leads to valuable work, it has to be recognized that involvement and absorption are not always achieved readily, or indeed at all with some children. To ignore this, or to treat occasions when children do not become involved as total failures, is dangerous and misleading for a number of reasons. If the teacher is led to regard involvement or absorption as a prerequisite of useful work:

1 He will regard its absence as some kind of personal failure.
2 He will be tempted to devise a repertoire of cheap tricks whereby this condition of involvement may apparently be attained.
3 He will become preoccupied with those types of activity in which involvement is apparently easier to achieve—solo work at the expense of group work, exploratory work at the expense of expressive—forgetting, meanwhile, that involvement is a means to an end rather than the end itself.

### 3.2.2 A positive approach

In order to redress this particular balance, therefore, it is necessary to stress the importance of *concentration*. By whatever means seem suitable, children need to be shown that there is a problem *and* a way of solving it: when absorption does not happen as freely as we might like, then we can fall back on deliberate mental attitudes towards the work that will produce useful results. The lesson extract quoted in 3.2.1 showed a fairly natural way in which a class became aware that their work would be hampered by their awareness of the people around them. A continuation of such a lesson would be to point out to the children that John's awareness of all the people watching him meant that he wasn't thinking enough about the old man and his problems. If the class then all work simultaneously at the activity, a major part of the feeling of being exposed will be removed at a stroke.

There is another, more direct method that is suitable for some classes. The teacher asks for a volunteer from the class and, if possible, the most confident member of the class is chosen. The other children are then invited to stare at the volunteer, possibly with further encouragement from the teacher (such as 'Look at his face; look at his hands,' and so on). When the volunteer appears thoroughly embarrassed, as normally happens, he is then questioned as to how he feels, with attention paid to his physical sensations—hot face, peculiar feelings in the stomach, trembling legs, and so on. He is then asked why he felt like that, and will normally reply that it was because everyone was staring at him. When the teacher has got as much out of this questioning as possible, he then casually asks the volunteer to perform some small task for him (re-arrange some rostra, fetch some chairs, or clean the blackboard). This is done in such a way as to appear totally unrelated to what has gone before. When the task has been completed, the teacher calls the child back and asks how he felt while doing it. Did he feel as he felt before? Normally the answer will be that he felt perfectly all right. How can this be? The class were still looking at him, weren't they? Yes, they were. Then why didn't he feel embarrassed? The answer is that he had something to put his mind to, something to do.

Whether this method or some other is used, there are two important lessons to be pointed out: that drama will involve concentrating on the 'something you have to do'; and that such concentration is voluntary and involves an act of the will. How these points operate in practice will be treated shortly, but the second of them is worth emphasizing because it is a major link between conventional classroom lessons and their controls and the relatively unconventional demands that drama makes.

No doubt in an ideal world every drama lesson would be so imaginatively conceived and gripping that the children would soon be totally absorbed in imaginative activity. However, this does not always happen, and we have to be grateful when it does and prepared for the occasions when it does not. There will be times when children come to drama for the first time and see it as a glorious opportunity to relax from 'real' lessons for a while. Drama is indeed a relaxation but not in the sense such an attitude implies. It has to be made clear, therefore, that drama is, in its own way, more demanding than other subjects, not less, that it has its own working discipline, and that what takes place in the lesson depends on the attitudes of those taking part. There is no mystery about it, in other words, and those who want to enjoy drama and work successfully at it can do so. The problems can be overcome by anyone with interest and determination. This needs saying because inexperienced teachers will often blame themselves for a failure with a child who is simply determined not to get involved and participate. There are naughty children here as anywhere else: classroom drama is neither magic nor religion and cannot be blamed for failure to conjure or convert.

### Exclusion exercises
The basis of these exercises is that the actor attempts to complete some

activity in the presence of a variety of distractions. A large number of such exercises have been devised[2] and individuals can easily adapt or invent their own. Those that follow are thus only examples.

*Pair conversation*
The children divide into pairs. They are given a topic to talk about, which should be simple enough to allow them to talk freely and without too much careful thought (for example, 'TV programmes I watched last night', 'Things I hate'). They are then instructed to face each other, to look each other in the eye, and at a given signal to start talking, both at the same time. They must not shout, look away, laugh, or stop. If either does, then both must stop and remain silent. This introduces a competitive element to see which pair continues talking for the longest time without breaking down.

*Variations*    If the pair breaks down, then both must stop, regain concentration, and then start again.

While continuing the exercise as originally described, both must attempt to pick up the gist of what their partner is saying. At the end of the conversation they then compare notes.

*Truth and lies*
The class is again divided into pairs. The pairs first of all decide which of them shall question and which shall answer. The questions may be of any general kind. The questioner begins by asking a question, which his partner answers truthfully. Another question is asked, but this time the answer must be untrue. The third question is answered truthfully, the fourth untruthfully, and so on. There must be no other conversation, each must look at the other all the time, and there must be no laughing.

*Variations*    It may be useful to have a practice beforehand in which all the answers are untrue.

Repeat the original exercise, with the variation that, to begin with, all answers are truthful until a signal is given (for example, a cymbal clash), and then they are all untruthful, until the next signal, and so on.

## *One against the group*

The basic exercise here is similar to 'pair conversation'. The class is divided into groups, or may work as one large group. One person is chosen and stands with the rest of the group round him. He gives a talk on some relatively simple topic and the others attempt to destroy his concentration by asking him questions on unrelated subjects. Every time a question is asked, the speaker has to stop, answer the question, and then continue his talk without pausing or repeating himself.

*Variations*   The speaker reads a passage from a book and after each question has to return to the word he had reached, without marking his place in any way.

The speaker recites a passage learned by heart.

Instead of asking questions, the rest of the group may use any 'reasonable' means to distract the speaker.


## Intentness exercises

Simple intentness exercises can be based on the senses of hearing, sight, and touch (the other two senses are rather too difficult to work on in the classroom). Again, the exercises that follow are only examples.


## *Sounds around*

The children sit or lie with eyes closed, and concentrate on hearing, and listing mentally, all the sounds they can hear. These are recalled afterwards with the help of detailed questions from the teacher.

*Variations*   The children are instructed to ignore all the sounds outside the room.

The children are instructed to ignore all the sounds inside the room.


## *Sound sequence*

The children relax as before, with eyes closed. The teacher moves round the room making a series of noises—banging a radiator, rattling the curtains, and so on. He then repeats the sequence with a number of small alterations. The children have to identify these.

*Variations*   A tape of sound effects is used instead of live sounds.

A passage is read from a book instead, and repeated with variations as before.

## Looking

Children concentrate their attention on one object in the room. They then close their eyes and attempt to re-create the object in their mind's eye. They open their eyes and check their mental image for accuracy.

*Variations*   Done without preliminary concentration on an object. The teacher tells the class to shut their eyes and visualize a particular object in the room, which he names. Checking as before.

Done with an object not in the room (for example, 'your own front door').

Children in pairs. One shuts his eyes. The other names an object and the first has to describe it in as much detail as possible.

## Touching

*Pair work*   One shuts his eyes and has to identify a small object handed him by the other.

*Blind man*   Children in pairs take it in turns to guide each other round the room. No speaking. At the end of the exercise, the 'blind man' has to work out where he is and where he has been. Best done with blindfolds.

*Crossing the room*   Room arranged with obstacles spaced across the middle. Children are individually given the task of crossing the room blindfold unaided (the teacher must be on hand to avoid the possibility of accident).

## Object memory

In groups. An object is handed from one person to another along a line. The last man puts it down and then picks it up again *in mime*. It is then passed in mime back along the line.

## Developments

The exercises that have been described may be used in isolation (and some can profitably fill in odd moments of other lessons). Equally, however, they can lead to further work within the scope of one lesson. Whichever is done, the way in which the exercises relate to other work needs to be clearly demonstrated. Although some of them are quite clearly games, they are games with a serious purpose, and if this purpose is understood they will be played with enthusiasm as well as enjoyment, and later work will benefit. One of the easiest ways in which links with other work can be shown is to develop a more realistic situation directly from a game, as in the following example.

*'The gossip'*

1 'Pair conversation' is played as described above.
2 At the end of the exercise the teacher asks the class about this kind of behaviour in real life. When some examples have been elicited, he sets up a situation between two people, both of whom talk all the time and never listen. It is often useful to get from the class some ideas about what sort of things such people tend to talk about, so that those who are short of ideas needn't feel embarrassed or at a loss. The conversation is then begun, after a reminder that if it breaks down, they should stop, regain concentration, and then start again.
3 After this conversation, the teacher asks the class their opinions of the character of such people, continuing the discussion long enough for plenty of ideas again to be available. The pairs then cast themselves as 'A' and 'B' in the following situation. A is just a gossip. B is much quieter and less assertive. Yet they are friends. On this occasion, B has some very important news to give A ('No, B, don't discuss it, just decide for yourself'). A, of course, goes on talking about nothing and not listening as usual. The conversation is then repeated.
4 This time the teacher asks the children how they feel when talking to such a person. What happens if you really have got something important to say and the other person just never listens? From the discussion which follows it will probably be possible to develop the idea of some kind of climax with which the scene ends (for example, B loses his temper and storms off). Participants should be left to devise their own endings to the scene. Scenes do not always develop to a climax like this, but occasions when they do not are also worth discussing. (There may be

good reasons within the situation for it not ending as the teacher expects it to.)

## 3.3 Class atmosphere and class work

So far we have concentrated in this chapter on the problems to be faced in the classroom. Obviously the teacher should not go into a class looking for problems, that may not in fact exist, but rather he should set out with the aim of establishing the right kind of working atmosphere from the start.

The first step in establishing an appropriate atmosphere is to ensure that the subject-matter to be treated is seen by both pupils and teacher as important and relevant to them now. The major defect of much of the 'old' English was that passages, poems, and books studied were either trivial or remote. In drama, too, it is easy to misjudge the class and choose material that is trivial because too young, or boring because too remote from the social or imaginative experience of the children. The teacher then has to ensure that the pupils feel they can talk about it honestly and with confidence. This is not always easy to achieve, especially in schools where pupils are not encouraged to articulate their experiences and opinions. The process may be a slow one, involving a long period of work in small groups before discussion in full class can take place—if it ever can (see 7.5). If this confidence never grows, however, there will be a serious limit to the progress that can be made. Discussion of behaviour in social interactions can be a sensitive business, and if pupils feel that they are in danger of being laughed at, however mildly or surreptitiously, then their exploration and analysis will remain superficial.

The pupils also need help in developing confidence in each other in practical work. Much of the initial work will be done either solo, with all the class working at the same time, or in pairs. If children are allowed to choose their own partners and then work for a period of time with the same person, there will be adequate opportunity for such confidence to develop. Also, by working in *ad hoc* groups, both large and small, children will get used to working with many other members of the class and to contributing and sharing ideas. Two useful ways of introducing such work are crowd scenes and contribution scenes.

### 3.3.1 Crowd scenes

**Unfocused crowd scenes**

It is very useful to devise an occasion or a situation in which a wide variety of different people would meet and interact naturally. The whole class can then participate without any more structuring or control than is offered by the situation itself. The children choose their own character or role and then participate as fully as they feel confident to do. The main structure is normally offered by a combination of place and occasion—for example, railway station at rush hour, market at midday, fairground at night. The rough details of different locations are sketched in and a short class discussion will develop a number of ideas about the kind of people likely to be around and the reasons for their presence. Children are then asked to choose a character, decide why they are there (and possibly where they have come from and where they are going). The teacher then starts the activity, possibly covering any awkwardness with a record of suitable 'busy' music. The degree to which the children become active in the scene then depends upon them. So, too, does the extent to which they decide to make their character relate to the other characters present. Initially it is usually as well to keep such scenes fairly short and to 'leave them alone', although it is, of course, possible to develop them by class discussion. Such discussion, however, must be concentrated on the scene as a whole, and on the corporate nature of the effort, rather than on the criticism of the contribution of any particular individual. 'How can we get more of a rush-hour atmosphere?' and 'Do you think we ought to have more customers and fewer stall-holders?' are the kind of questions one might expect to ask.

**Focused crowd scenes**

The crowd scene can be developed further by the introduction of one or more incidents which will serve to focus the scene dramatically:

1 A shouted instruction from a teacher.
For example, 'Here is an announcement. It has just been learned that there are skilful pickpockets at large in the market.'
2 Intervention by the teacher as a character.
For example, At the fair he suddenly accuses one of the characters of stealing his money.

3  Introduction of a pre-planned 'happening'.
For example, the teacher arranges with two of the boys that at a signal
from him a fight will break out at the fair.

### 3.3.2 Contribution scenes

The above crowd scenes are very useful, but they sometimes fail to
provide much practice for actors playing together, and sometimes even
encourage them to play against each other. To encourage pupils to work
together, a series of exercises can be used, in which actors are gradually
added to a scene and contribute what they can to it. In some versions
they actually modify the scene they enter. Some examples follow.

**'Add to the activity'**
One actor goes to the centre and begins a simple and clear piece of
occupational mine (for example, doing the washing-up after a large
meal). The teacher then points to another actor and without any discussion he has to work out what is being done and then join in, either
helping with the original activity or starting another one that could be
occurring in the same place (for example, making coffee). This process
continues with further actors being added. The exercise can be varied
by the use of speech within the scene, provided there is no discussion
about what people are doing, but only talk that arises out of the situation.

**'Add to the relationship'**
The spoken version of the exercise above is played, but this time each
new actor assumes a relationship to one or more of those already in the
scene. Again, this is not to be explicit, but must be perceptible in the
general conduct of the actor. The other actors have to work out the
relationships while continuing with the scene.

**'What are you doing there?'**
This exercise is similar to the previous one except that the first actor
decides nothing. He merely stands or sits in the centre. The second

actor decides place, time, both characters, and the relationship. The first
actor has to work out what these are as quickly as possible from what
the second says and does. Other actors can be added later as in the other
exercises.


## 3.4 Working space

Communicative behaviour uses the body as well as the voice, and cannot
be properly explored if there are unnatural physical constraints imposed
by restricted space. Particular schools will provide space in a variety of
ways. Sometimes the hall is suitable; occasionally there is a purpose-
built studio. More frequently an existing room has to be adapted, and
in schools where rooms are allocated by subject there is no reason why
one of the English rooms could not be given over to improvised drama,
spoken work, and discussions.

The primary need is for adequate, uncluttered floor space. The most
elaborate equipment in the world will not really help in a cramped classroom full of desks. The work upon which much of this book is based
was done in a room 35' by 28', in which the only furniture was a set of
rostra high enough to be used as seats, about a dozen chairs, and two
tables, one of which usually held equipment, and the other of which
served as a prop table in scenes. This amount of space is just about
enough for secondary pupils to do most improvised work, but when we
wanted to concentrate on any vigorous movement we had to move to
the assembly hall, which was already under pressure from the music
and P.E. departments. Any classroom can in fact be used for a wide
range of work, provided that the desks can be removed from the room.

Obviously one wants as little furniture as possible, or rather, one
wants furniture that takes up as little space as possible when not in use.
Enough chairs for every pupil to be able to sit down can be stacked in a
relatively small space. A few portable rostra can be very useful in providing different levels, for denoting different acting areas, for turning into
market stalls, broken-down lorries, cafe tables, and so on. They can also
be used as seats, to keep the number of chairs down. The only other
essential item of 'furniture' in my opinion is some provision whereby
children are prevented from bringing clutter into the working area with
them. There is no point in providing a beautifully uncluttered floor
space if, as soon as the class come in, it is going to be covered with

textbooks, folders, furry pencil cases, and tins of rock cakes from the domestic science lesson. Shelving outside the working area can help to deal with this problem.

## 3.5 Equipment

A record player and mains tape-recorder are more or less essential. Their principal uses are in the provision of music and other sound stimuli and for the recording of pupils' work (see 9.5 and 9.6). Cassette recorders are extremely useful when pupils are developing their own work (see 8.4.1). Video-recording equipment and the use of a closed-circuit television camera are dealt with in the Appendix.

Blackout and stage lighting can be useful in two ways:

1 They can be used to provide atmosphere by the use of colour, light, and shade (with the provisos noted in 2.1).
2 They can mark off a performance area for work on the expressive function of drama (that is, with light on the actors and off the audience).

Stage lights are, however, large, fairly fragile, and expensive to replace, and their use in an adapted classroom has problems (especially of safety and of the provision of an adequate power supply). The teacher should consider carefully whether they are really going to be useful and then *consult either his L.E.A. Drama Adviser or some other qualified person about the practicalities.* Further general information and advice on types of equipment and methods of use can always be obtained from the L.E.A. English or Drama Adviser.

## Notes

1 It is, perhaps, worth suggesting one reason why many of the books written on the subject have been somewhat starry-eyed about the school situation. A good three-quarters of the teachers' books listed in Chapter 10 were written by people out of immediate touch with regular school-teaching experience: most are college lecturers or drama advisers and many have reached their positions via the theatre rather than schools. Such people inevitably have a different view of school life from the regular teacher, and even when they work with children in school, they

do not get an experience that is truly comparable with that of the ordinary classroom teacher. They are not under the same pressure from the timetable as the teacher—being chased round the school building seven times a day by the school bell with inadequate time for marking or preparation and extreme personal demands from children. They do not stand as representatives of the institution and therefore children do not come to their lessons with the same pre-conceptions. Their classes thus take place in a completely different and artificial context and any principles which are drawn from them must be treated with considerable caution.

2  Examples will be found in Spolin (1963), Hodgson and Richards (1966), Way (1967), and Bowskill (1973b).

# 4

# The elements: defining situations

## 4.1 The first four elements

Much of the shoddy and shapeless work that one sees in children's
improvised drama comes from a lack of understanding by their teachers
of the true nature of the activity. There is a lot of pointless, and sometimes dangerous, indulgence in emotion for its own sake. Of course,
emotion has its place in the improvised situation, just as it does in the
real-life interaction which it simulates, but it is not the sole, or even the
most important part of the improvisation. First of all childen need to
understand, explicitly or implicitly, that all social interactions have
certain general structural similarities and that these must always be
present in an improvisation. A linguistic analysis of these features was
begun in Chapter 1 and will be extended in Chapter 6, but at this stage
in the practical work, we need only to distinguish four simple elements:

place
time
character
relationship.

Children should be conscious that all of these are present in any improvisation, that they normally need to be established before the improvisation begins, and that when it breaks down, or is only partly successful,
then frequently the reason can be located in one of these four elements.
  Because these elements are so important, it is useful to work on them
separately both before work on full situations begins at all and also as a
preliminary to work on a specific situation or group of situations. The
general principles underlying preparatory work on the elements of place,
time, character, and relationship are discussed in 4.2, after each of them
has been considered separately in more detail.

45

In context

## 4.1.1 Place

The influence of place on improvisation can be explored through:

1 Boundaries
Large and small spaces; physical confinement; tunnels, cages, caves; finding out the extent of a room in the dark; imaginary boundaries in a large space.
2 Entrances
Where? What kind of entrance (door, gate, bead curtain, triumphal arch)? What is on the other side? How do we feel about that in anticipation? How do we open the door? How do we walk through?
3 Related spaces
Rooms next door; the outside (garden, prison courtyard); passing through one room on the way to another. Where are you coming from? Where are you going to?
4 Contents
How the furniture determines the nature of the space; acting in a space with imaginary furniture in it; using different areas of the same space according to where the furniture is; use of small objects; relationship between objects.
5 Large spaces
Practice in using a lot of space; awareness of mental maps; effects of atmosphere (cathedral, bus station, sports arena).
6 Surface and terrain
Different surfaces (mud, cobbles, rock); effects on movement; different terrains (plain, mountain, desert, marsh); different means of progression (climbing, walking, crawling).

Early solo work on movement can concentrate on different and contrasting experiences of place, either as a series of short movement exercises, possibly using music, or linked together in some way (for example, based on a journey). Later work in pairs and groups can develop the realistic use of a limited space such as a room and concentrate more on naturalistic detail. Place can also be used as a unifying factor in connection with other elements. One way to build up a fairly free improvisation in which children work out character for themselves, but ignore relationship, is to choose a suitable setting—for example, a place where a wide range of characters would naturally assemble, but where they can also interact normally without any strong or unusual stimulus being necessary.

### 4.1.2 Time

Questions like those below will encourage the children to think about time:

What time of day? (Is it light or dark?)
What time of year? (What is the weather like?)
What happened before?
What is going to happen next?
How long have we got?

Again, solo exercises can be separate or linked together. One useful exercise is to ask all five questions about one simple action or movement. First, the children have to decide individually why they should be doing this particular action at this particular time, and how the time context affects the movement. After the movement is done, the same questions are asked, about the same movement, but this time different answers have to be supplied, and the movement is performed again, with these answers in mind.

### 4.1.3 Character

Only the more obvious features which will affect the portrayal of character are indicated here.

1 Solo movement can concentrate on: age, temperament, occupation, physical characteristics, home background.
2 Imagination can be stimulated by: the use of music, the use of un-usual, imaginative, or humorous names, the provision of one small detail with instructions to the children to fill in the rest of the details.
3 In pair conversations, further characteristics can be added: accent (social, regional, national); vocal characteristics (high/low, fast/slow).

There should be progression from very caricatured role types towards more sophisticated and individually defined characters.

### 4.1.4 Relationship

In preparatory work the children need to be shown what is meant by 'relationship' and what the practical factors affecting it are.

1 History
What is the background to the relationship? How long have the people been acquainted? Has the relationship followed a consistent pattern? Has it been very erratic? What major personal events have affected it?
2 Emotional tone
Is there a consistent emotional tone which shows itself in transactions between the characters? Is much emotion displayed at all? Is emotion deliberately being concealed? For what reason?
3 Roles
Are the characters involved in a professional role relationship? What is their social role relationship? Does one character consistently dominate the relationship?

As with character, a particularly effective way of introducing these concepts is by the use of a series of small-scale pair conversations in which a number of relationships can be 'experimented with' in a short space of time.

## 4.2 Progressive work on the elements

Generally speaking, the following principles will govern the progression of preliminary work on the elements of a situation.

1 Solo → pair → group
Solo work, to help develop concentration, can easily lead into pair work, to develop material. Pairs can then combine into fours or sixes to develop the skill of playing together in a situation.
2 Movement → speech
Particularly with younger children, it is usually easier to begin without speech and only to use situations involving talking when confidence has been developed.
3 Broad → subtle
The obvious, the exaggerated, and the humorous are easier to cope with early on than situations involving careful thought, sensitivity, and subtlety of imagination.

4  Situation ⟶ concept
Generally one begins with concrete situations designed to allow the class
to experience the element involved, only later working on the concept
in a more theoretical way.


## 4.3 The fifth element: the problem

So far in this chapter the emphasis has been upon those elements of an
everydaysocial interaction that must also be present in an improvisation.
Just as place and time affect my social behaviour, and my judgement of
my role and relationship with other people affects my language and
physical behaviour in everyday interactions, so too must the actor have
answers to the questions 'Where?', 'When?', 'Who?', and 'What relationship?' before embarking upon an improvisation. This information on its
own, however, is not enough to develop a worthwhile improvised situation. We may concentrate on specific linguistic and paralinguistic behaviour, or our attention may be on role, role-relationship, or group
membership, but, whatever the intention, it is necessary to feed something more into the situation before work is begun. The improvisation
has to be more than merely a simulated social interaction in order to
focus and concentrate the attention of those taking part on whatever
may be the particular area of study.
    An example will help to make this clear. Suppose we wish to con-
sider the role relationship between the adolescent and his parent. We
might then outline the four elements as follows:

place (the living room)
time (late evening)
characters (father, mother, teenage son)
relationships (parents get on very well together, but recently they have
experienced difficulties in their relationship with their only son).

If that is all the information we were to give the group working on the
situation, then whether or not anything worthwhile emerged would be
largely a matter of chance. We might well end up with an accurately
simulated social interaction, possibly containing a certain amount of
bickering that many might consider typical of the situation as described,
but it is relatively unlikely that anything really useful would be learned
about teenage/parent relationships. For this to happen, we need to focus

the attention of the characters upon a particular problem and to put them under some kind of pressure. We can do this by giving the actors further instructions as follows:

Parents
You are generally concerned that your son has been staying out rather late recently and today you learned that he has been seen wandering aimlessly round the streets draped round a rather scruffy-looking girl.
Son
You are fed up with home because your parents are far too strict. Recently got a new girl-friend and this evening been up to the youth club disco with her and had a great time.
Everyone
It is 11.30 p.m.—an hour after the son said he would be home. The scene begins as the parents hear him open the front door.

By doing this we have defined the situation in two main ways. First, we have delineated a specific area of the relationship to be explored—the parent/son relationship when it is challenged by the demands of growing up, of adolescent socialization. Specifically, too, we may be looking at the relationship between mother and son when it is called into question by the competition of a girl-friend. Secondly, there is now a definite starting point (coming in late) that will provide the spark to set the situation off and help the participants to avoid the temptation of 'talking round' the situation without ever really getting into it.

The fifth element that has to be provided, therefore, is the 'problem'.[1] The problem sets a dramatic situation apart from a simple simulated interaction. It is defined in such a way that those involved are led to concentrate on the specific area of study. As a result, too, it should be possible for them to bring the resultant conflict to some sort of climax and even resolution. This will not always happen, of course. The problem may be avoided, or the definition may not be accurate enough to focus the improvisation as much as the teacher hopes. Defining the problem upon which a situation is based is one of the most difficult things in this kind of teaching: make your definiton too detailed and either half of it will be forgotten, or it will stifle all initiative and imagination; make it too vague and you succeed only in setting up a 'talk-shop'. As with many things in the classroom, success comes with experience and is dependent upon the teacher's ability to define clearly what his particular objectives are.

## Notes

1  It should be noted that the word 'problem' is not being used here as it is by a writer such as Spolin (1963) who uses it to apply to problems that are essentially theatrical and have to be solved by actors. In this chapter and elsewhere the word is used to describe problems that derive from *life* and have to be solved by *characters*.

# 5

# Classwork: setting up a situation

In the use of the improvised situation as a basis for lessons, we may distinguish three main phases, which together make up one unit:

preliminary work
performance
discussion.

## 5.1 Preliminary work

The purpose of preliminary work is twofold: to introduce the class to the subject-matter in hand and to prepare them to explore it in dramatic terms. How a particular situation is introduced will depend on a number of factors: how much work has been done on the theme or story of which the situation forms a part; whether similar characters, relationships, or problems have been tackled before; where in the lesson (or the term or the course) the unit comes; and so on. Thus a first year class with little or no experience of improvised drama, just starting on a new theme, will probably have to spend several lessons on preliminary work because improvisation itself and the subject matter are both new. A specialist third or fourth year group, however, can probably drop straight into performance with little more than a few words of explanation and a moment or two for thought.

The main activities involved in preliminary work are:

explanation by the teacher and class discussion
preliminary practical work
planning by pairs and groups.

Sometimes all these steps may be necessary, but more often one or more may be omitted.

## 5.1.1 Explanation and discussion

### Explanation by the teacher

Unfortunately even experienced drama teachers often confuse pupils by the vagueness of their instructions. The pupil may then feel that his own confusion is exceptional and that drama involves activities and mental attitudes that he will never master. The teacher must state clearly to the class what the subject-matter is, and what he wants them to do. Basically they need to know two things:

1  What is the situation about?
Who are the characters? What is their relationship? What is their relevant history? What are the place and time? What is the problem?
2  What do we have to do?
Have we to decide the answer to any of those questions ourselves? Where do we start? Where do we finish? How do we decide who plays which part? What do we do when we've finished?

### Discussion

It is frequently, although not always, useful to begin a lesson with discussion. Certainly where work is being related to a theme, such as the project 'Moneytime' quoted on p. 108, discussion is important. Where several situations are worked through in one lesson, then some kind of discussion will automatically be interposed between situations:

preliminary work
↓
performance
↓
discussion
↓
preliminary work
↓
performance
↓
discussion
↓
preliminary work
↓

In this case, analytical discussion and preliminary work for the next situation will naturally merge into each other.

The discussion serves two purposes in introducing a situation: it arouses interest and it brings relevant experience to bear on the subject matter. The lesson extract in 2.2 came from such a discussion. All the elements of a dramatic exploration are here waiting to be organized into a situation by the teacher. The class, by means of lively talk, have brought their own relevant experience to the front of their minds ready for use in action. At this preliminary stage, the discussion is concerned largely with the subject-matter ('life') rather than the nature of the dramatic activity ('art').

### 5.1.2 Preliminary practical work

The last chapter suggested how preliminary practical work might be tackled to explore place, time, character and relationship in connection with a particular situation. This can be done solo, or in pairs, or in small groups. As well as serving to concentrate attention on the elements of a situation, such work also provides a useful 'way in' to the main work on the situation.

### Solo
If the class is inexperienced, or the subject-matter new, a certain amount of solo work on movement may be necessary as an introduction. If a situation involves some conflict between two participants, solo work on the production of an accurate mime of some specific activity in a particular place may provide a useful framework. Observation of how that mime alters when affected by a specific mood may well help the children over initial problems of concentration, character, and emotion. Similarly, solo work may be concentrated on a particular occupation or age group. This may lead straight into the dramatic situation, or prepare for further preliminary work in pairs or groups.

### In pairs or groups
It is often useful to 'work round' a situation rather than attack it straight on. If, for example, a situation is rather emotional and very close to the

pupil's own intimate experience—as many family situations are—then it can be difficult for the pupils to improvise if it is approached too abruptly. Suppose the teacher wishes to use a situation where a father has found out that his daughter has been seeing a boy he disapproves of. This is probably very close to home for many third and fourth year pupils, but it does raise important issues that need to be dealt with. The class could be prepared by pair work on the components of the scene as follows:

1 Work in boy/girl pairs
Perhaps the class has always worked in groups of the same sex. It would be foolish to start a new working method with such a difficult problem. Therefore a lot of preparatory work in fairly low key would be necessary.
2 Father/daughter relationship in general
There are several difficulties initially: the actors have to invent and live a long history to the relationship; girls may well not care to think about the relationship too much if they don't get on with their own father; boys may well find it next to impossible to imagine what it is like to be a father; and so on. Again, work on simpler situations such as arguing about pocket money, what time the daughter has to be in at night, and similar problems will help prepare for the main situation.
3 The nature of parental authority
The boy may find it difficult to impose that kind of authority that comes with the age and status of the character. If this happens, then the improvisation will not be about a father and daughter, but about a bossy boy and a recalcitrant girl. Here work on situations in which both take it for granted that the daughter will accept the father's authority will help.
4 Just talking about boyfriends ·
This may cause problems (of 'silliness') which may be broken down in different ways. The situation can be reversed so that the father is enthusing about a young man of the family's acquaintance and the daughter is expressing disapproval. This is an altogether lighter situation which leads well into the more serious one.[1]

How far such practical work in pairs is taken depends on the experience of the class and the desirability of extending the general work on the father/daughter relationship.

### 5.1.3 Planning by pairs and groups

At the beginning of a course, or of a new section of work, the teacher's instructions may be so specific that no further preparation by the pupils is required.

Increasingly, however, decisions about casting, time, place, and even character and relationship may be left to the actors. In this case, a certain amount of preparatory discussion will be necessary, but it should not take the form of preparing a mental scenario. Children should realize the significance of spontaneity in their work—after all we don't have a detailed scenario in problem situations in real life. Therefore, 'Don't decide how it ends, wait to see what happens', should be the attitude to such pre-planning. The teacher will need to listen in to the discussions from time to time to ensure that groups only prepare what is absolutely essential for a scene—place, time, character, relationship. The time allowed should be limited—often a bare sixty seconds will suffice.

## 5.2 Performance

The word 'performance' has two meanings that are relevant here: the execution of an action (in this case, the improvisation); and the execution of an action for the benefit of an audience.

If the improvisation is intended to be purely analytical, then the teacher will find that it is easier to base a discussion on a performance seen by all (usually after all groups have had a chance to run through the situation at the same time). Performance in front of the class can, however, still be dispensed with and the discussion based on the work done by separate pairs or groups. This is not quite as satisfactory, and is most suitable with a class who find concentration difficult.

Where the improvisation focuses on synthesis, the teacher has a choice. Initially, when the children are beginning to be absorbed in their work, and to explore the possibilities of a consistent personality, performance even in front of the class might be detrimental, and there is little need for it. They can all work on the situation at the same time. Once a class has got used to the work, however, it is sometimes valuable for them to share their experience by having volunteer groups perform their scene for the benefit of the rest of the class. The performance will not be quite the same as it was the first time, because it is a repeat, and therefore no longer strictly exploratory, and also because, however good their concentration, the performers will be aware of their audience.

Clearly if the aim is expression, then the class may have a period of work on their own, but performance in front of others is essential. The conditions of performance here are rather different and methods of organization are dealt with more specifically in Chapter 8.

For whatever purpose a piece of work is performed to an audience it is advisable to avoid a lot of fuss about the conditions of performance. This only causes a break in the flow of the lesson and allows time for the actors to get 'cold' and for their concentration to flag. Those performing should just be allowed to run through their situation with everyone else standing or sitting wherever they were when they finished going through their own piece. What follows is a short scene developed by two second year pupils after the discussion quoted in 2.2. The class was given the following instructions:

TEACHER Now decide who is A and who is B.
(*Brief discussion to establish this.*)
All right? Now this is the situation. A is the son or daughter. B is the father or mother. OK? A has run out of pocket money and wants more. You decide why.
(*Beginnings of discussion.*)
No, don't tell each other yet. B you're in a bad mood, right? Now B, you're sitting down reading the paper or something when A comes in. Ready? . . . No, let's start with quiet . . . . (*Waits for silence.*)
Right—off you go.

This was one of the scenes that ensued.

A 'Ullo dad, will you give me some extra pocket money this week?
B No.
A Oh go on.
B What you want it for?
A Just four bob extra.
B No. You tell me what you want it for.
A I ain't telling you what I want it for.
B Well, (*some words indecipherable on tape*) . . . it doesn't matter then.
A Oh go on.
B No
A You only give me ten pence a week you do.

B You ain't having any more.

A Most of the kids get about a pound a week.

B So what, you're not having any.

A Oh come on.

B I know why you want the money. You're going to the pictures, ain't you.

A No I'm not.

B Yes you are. You're going with a bird to the pictures.

A No I'm not.

B That's why you want some more money.

A No it ain't. Come on lets have it.

B No you're not having any.*

## 5.3 Discussion

At this stage the inexperienced teacher faces another problem: now that I've got them to do a scene or situation, what do I do with it? Is that all? Do I just say, 'Very good', or 'Not bad, but perhaps you can do better next time', and then move on to something else? Obviously there must be progression in drama work and discussion is part of this progression. The questioning and discussion should be designed to open the work up, demonstrate possibilities, and point the way to further work. Yet how does one do it?

Initially the teacher will need to ask a series of questions. Later children will develop the ability to pose the questions themselves, but to begin with the teacher must take the initiative. The questions will be of three kinds:

observation (what happened)
interpretation (what it meant and why it happened)
speculation (what might have happened or what could happen).

It is important to note that no comments are made about quality. Obviously the use of praise for efforts made is a standard part of teaching technique, but in questioning, or in the stimulation of a discussion, the teacher is not concerned with judgements about whether a scene was 'good' or not, but with the events of the scene.

### 5.3.1 Observation

Effective understanding of an interaction depends initially upon our ability to receive signals effectively. We need to *see* and *hear*.

1 We hear:
a linguistic sounds (phonology), which we interpret as words and sentences (lexis and grammar);
b paralinguistic sounds (vocal tone and sounds that are not words, such as 'ums' and 'aahs', which help us to interpret the speaker's precise intention).
2 We see:
gesture
facial expression
posture
body movement
eye movements.

All these contribute to the overall meaning of the situation.

When analysing an acted situation, therefore, the first thing we have to do is to concentrate the attention of the class on what the characters did and said. This may seem obvious, but surprisingly often even a trained observer will come away from a situation with a false impression of what actually happened. In the example quoted in 5.2, questioning could concentrate on the manner in which the son put his request and the way in which the father reacted. Even at this relatively early stage it is important to pin the class down to specifics:

Q *How* did the son ask for more pocket money?
A Politely.
Q Why do you say he was polite?
A Well, because of the way he asked.
Q What way?
A Well . . . you know . . . he asked him nicely.
Q Yes. Was his voice loud or quiet?
A Quiet.
Q How was he standing?
A Like this (*demonstrates*).
Q And that's a polite way of standing?
A Well . . . yes.

## 5.3.2 Interpretation

The class can then be led to consider the question of why the participants behaved as they did. This involves interpreting not just the literal meaning of what was said but also the gloss put on that meaning by intonation, facial expression, gesture, and so on, thus elaborating the total meaning of the situation. Motive will also need to be considered, and children will probably want to share their own experiences with the class.

In such discussion, two kinds of irrelevance may occur: children may begin to make judgements about the quality of the acting; and they may try to produce hypothetical cases to prove points ('Well, if he's misbehaved yesterday, then the father would have been angry.') What is wanted is an insistence on the use of evidence—what actually happened in the situation, and what the actual experience is of those taking part in the discussion. In the scene between father and son, questions to consider would be:

Why did the father refuse the boy?
What was the father's attitude to girl-friends?
Whose father would behave in this way?
Whose father would behave differently?
Why these differences?

Now, from this questioning and discussion, weaknesses may be revealed in the improvisation itself. It is clear to me, for instance, that B had not really thought out why he won't give A the money: in fact, his "stonewalling' attitude is, I suspect, more because of B's insecurity as an actor than because of the demands of the situation. In this case, it is useful to do further work on the same situation without going to the third stage of discussion. One might, for example, work in threes on two scenes:

1 Father and his friend discuss the unsatisfactory conduct of the son in general (thus detailing and fixing the reasons for the original refusal).
2 The father and son scene as before.

The interest of this second scene can be heightened if the actor playing the son is not aware of the complaints that the father makes to his friend.

### 5.3.3 Speculation

So far the questioning has been typical of other kinds of discussion work with children, and has followed logically from the original situation. The third stage of discussion, however, is more difficult to predict or discuss in general terms, because it depends heavily on the teacher's judgement of the class. The next situation, in fact, should develop from this part of the discussion in a way that is obvious to the children. Questioning can usefully focus on the following areas:

1 Context
What would happen if the scene took place somewhere else (for example, in the boy's bedroom, or in the street)? Or at a different time (for example, three minutes before the boy wanted to go out)?
2 Character and mood
What happens if we make the boy very shy, or very assertive? What happens if the father is in an unexpectedly good mood?
3 Relationship
Suppose that the boy and his father are always having rows about money? Or what if the boy normally gets on well with his mother and badly with his father?
4 Problem
Taking exactly the same context, character, mood, and relationship, what happens if the boy, instead of asking for more pocket money, asks to go away to a pop festival for a weekend?

### 5.3.4 The extent and function of discussion

How much importance discussion has in the overall lesson plan will depend on whether the teacher's primary concern is with exploration and synthesis, or analysis. If the former, then the function of discussion is to clarify in the children's minds what has been done and to develop from it the subject-matter of the next improvisation. If the latter, then of course the discussion will be longer and more detailed. Whichever is adopted, the organization of the discussion will be much the same as that of discussions in English or other lessons. It is important to remember that the function of the teacher is not to 'elicit' the 'right answer' but to lead children to make explicit their intuitive observations and judgements about the situation. We are seeking to develop certain kinds of awareness and judgement and in this field there are no right answers, only more and less sophisticated responses. The teacher, moreover, need only take a leading part in the discussion until the class have discovered the kind of questions that need to be asked. When that has happened he can retire to the role of chairman and will find increasingly that the third stage of discussion and the development of new situations will arise naturally from what the class want to talk about.

## 5.4 Development

Certain specific ways in which a situation can be developed from the speculative stage of discussion have already been suggested, and more complex forms of development are discussed in Chapters 6 and 7. The most suitable line of development for a particular class will depend on the children's experience and interests, but it is probably useful at this point to list briefly some of the criteria which will affect any development.

### 5.4.1 Criteria

**Dramatic**

This means basically what the class can cope with as a result of its experience of drama (and is not the same, obviously, as the stage of emotional or intellectual development). A very simple situation—such as a discussion between father and daughter about going out with a boyfriend—may be treated in a dramatically complex way. (For example, the father arrives in girl's room just as she is putting the phone down after a conversation with a boy who has invited her out. She thinks she knows the boy but isn't sure. During the conversation with her father she is partly attending to what he says and partly looking in a mirror trying to decide what hairstyle she wants for the date.) Thus one way of developing a situation is to extend it dramatically by increasing the complexity and sophistication of what the actors actually have to do.

**Emotional**

The stage of emotional development reached will affect the type of material used: clearly the father/daughter situation outlined above would not really be suitable until the boyfriend/girlfriend relationship has become a serious preoccupation. Another way of developing a situation is just to increase the emotional content of the scene, although this has to be treated with some caution.

**Intellectual**

The intellectual development of the children will also affect the content of ideas in a situation. The children should not be burdened with intellectual concepts that are foreign or difficult when they are already coping with material that is emotionally or dramatically difficult. Equally, there is no value in offering intelligent and experienced children a diet of intellectual pap.

### 5.4.2 An example worked through

It is important, therefore, that too many complications are not added at the same time; and it is necessary to be able to distinguish the source of difficulty when an improvisation goes wrong. If we look at the work of the class already quoted throughout this chapter, we can see how this works in practice.

They were working on the theme of parents and children and the unit quoted was the first. The children had relatively little experience of dramatic activity of the disciplined kind I am describing. They were rather limited intellectually but showed signs of emotional maturity beyond the general level of their year. As a result of these considerations, the work developed in the following way.

1  The son discusses his parents with a friend and tries to borrow money from him (pair work).
2  Performance and further discussion.
3  Discussion about 'kids' between parent and friend.
4  Performance and discussion.
5  Group work involving grandparent, parent, parent's friend, child, child's friend.

a Parent and friend discuss younger generation in general and own children in particular.
b They are joined by grandparent who has strong views on the subject.
c Child and friend discuss what to do next Saturday and make their plans.
d Child confronts parent with plan.

This final scene was in fact the whole point of the second part of the lesson. Since the original 'pocket money' scene had shown weaknesses of dramatic structure and emotional superficiality, it was necessary to have the intervening conversation pieces with friends in order to develop sufficient relevant material and to provide a convincing dramatic context. In the terms originally given at the start of the chapter, therefore, there were only two 'situations' and the variation between them was essentially one of subject matter. Items 1, 3, 5, and 5(a) were in fact 'preliminary practical work' since they did not in fact contain any specific problem. This shows how improvisation can be used analytically, while at the same time developing scenes and situations as parts of an overall story.

## 5.5 Lesson planning

Whatever the purpose of improvisation, the basic unit of work is the imaginary situation. The diagram on p. 65 tabulates the possible components of one situation 'unit'. Such a unit could take up quite a short section of one lesson, or could itself comprehend a number of lessons. The chapters that follow will suggest ways in which situation units can be developed and extended in a number of different ways.

## Notes

1 Examples of improvisations on the boyfriend/girlfriend theme may be found in 7.1.3 and 7.2.

# Class: setting up a situation

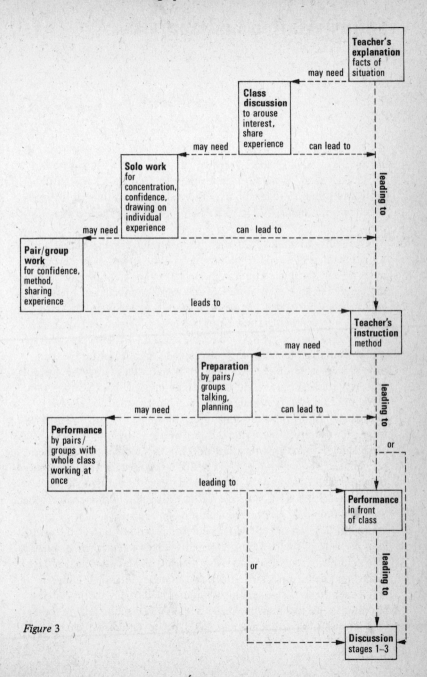

*Figure* 3

# 6
# Improvisation and analysis

It was suggested in Chapter 1 that an important part of linguistic and social inadequacy stems from an inability to distinguish sufficiently between different situation types. The young wife could not distinguish between situations sufficiently to deal properly with the housing official.

The ability to identify situations is obviously very important. It is something that develops as we grow up and the extent of its development is heavily dependent upon the social environment in which we mature. Some are clearly fortunate and gain a wide range of social experience, while others are disadvantaged. It would seem that such privilege and deprivation may be of two types, inter-related but capable of being distinguished. First, some children and young people clearly lead lives that are socially much broader and more adventurous than others. They experience life in city, town, and village; they meet people with very different jobs and from a variety of social backgrounds; they travel to other countries and (far more important than mere travel) participate in the life of the community they are visiting. (It is difficult to see, for example, that a fish-and-chip queue is any more or less socially broadening in Barcelona than in Baldock.) At the other extreme there are children who experience none of this social breadth at all and indeed to whom such experience is inconceivable. The second type of privilege and deprivation concerns the manner in which situations are approached. Some children may well be brought into contact with a range of situations but be conditioned by their parents' attitudes to treat them with large measure of similarity. If the parents perceive a number of situations (for example, all situations involving officials and money—post offices, banks, rent-collectors, council offices) as similar, then their children may be led to do the same. This is not confined to any particular class. Middle-class parents may put their children under such pressure to behave always in ways that are considered 'polite' or 'correct' that they scarcely dare to act at all and certainly do not fully exploit opportunities to gain new social experience because of a deep-rooted fear of making some unpardonable social error. If a person is conditioned in this way by his upbringing, then a range of situations that might be clearly distinct to others will appear to be blurred together by a general response of 'I-must-make-sure-that-I-don't-put-a-foot-wrong'.

The improvised situation has thus a fundamental part to play in extending the student's awareness of different situations and the meanings that are possible. This *analytical* use of improvisation takes place both through the practical experiment with role and context and in the subsequent discussion of what is revealed. How explicit and theoretical the teacher makes such work depends on his assessment of the needs and capabilities of his class. What is clear is that in order to be effective he needs an adequate theoretical framework himself. This will cover three main areas:

1 Register
The way in which different situation-types open up meaning possibilities, and the linguistic forms that these can take.
2 Paralanguage
The extra-linguistic aspects of communicative behaviour and the ways in which these affect our interpretation of the situation as a whole.
3 Presentation of self
The ways in which the different people involved in a situation define it and their role within it, and then seek to impose these definitions on the other participants.

## 6.1 Register

### 6.1.1 Defining the situation

Halliday's analysis of situations has already been referred to (1.1). If we examine this in more detail, we will see that it has considerable value for the teacher, both in the preparation of teaching material and in the discussion of classroom improvisation.

Halliday suggested that there were three 'dimensions' to a situation:
1 Field
where the interaction takes place
when the interaction takes place

67

what physical activities may be happening
the subject-matter about which the participants are communicating.
2 Tenor
the social roles of the participants and their role relationship.
3 Mode
the linguistic roles of the participants
the role of language itself in the situation.

### Field

1 'Where' may be defined in *geographical* terms ('at the summit of Snowdon', 'on a motorway service station forecourt'); in *personal/ physical* terms or *personal/emotional* terms ('in a very cold bus-shelter', 'in a spooky churchyard'); in *social* terms ('in a crowded transport cafe', 'at the counter of an expensive jeweller's'); or in some combination of these that may relate to the other variables.
2 'When' may be defined *chronologically* (that is, by the hour of the day, the date, the year); *seasonally* (summer, winter, rain, shine— relating to 'Where' of indoors/outdoors); in terms of the *relationship* involved ('It is a week after you told her you wanted to see her again'); in terms of other relevant variables ('It is just after the grave- yard gates have been closed for the night and the sexton has just been attacked by an IRA gang who are making good their escape').
3 'Subject-matter' is self-explanatory; it is 'what the characters talk about'. But it is often unnecessary to explain what the subject-matter is to a group. Once the other variables have been determined they can often be left to determine for themselves what it is that they have got to talk about.

### Tenor

1 'Social role' may be defined in terms of *family position* (son, father); *job* (teacher, bank manager); *group membership* (gang leader, cricket captain); *economic status* (a millionaire, a person buying a suit); broad *social status* (an aristocrat, a middle-class person); or some combination of these.
2 'Role relationship' is partly implied by social role (bank manager and client). In addition it is often defined *historically* in terms of what has gone on between the two before this particular interaction takes place ('This teacher has been having trouble with this pupil . . . .').

## Mode

1 'Linguistic role' is defined be describing the main way in which each participant is seeking to use language ('to persuade', 'to argue', 'to explain').

2 'The role of language', or the part that language plays in the whole situation, may be large or small. In a gang hold-up of a bank, for example, language may play very little part, while in a trial scene its part is much larger. Normally the determining of the other variables in a situation will decide what part language plays, but it is possible, and sometimes useful, to plan its role specifically ('Two prisoners planning an escape during a recreation-time conversation that is being monitored

## A situation defined

| Teacher's instructions | Variable |
| --- | --- |
| This is a scene for a girl and a boy. The boy is a private soldier and . . . . | social role A |
| the girl works in an inn. | social role B |
| She is his girlfriend. | role relationship |
| They are in the stable of the inn. | where |
| It is late at night and . . . | when |
| they are not supposed to be together. | (relevant part of field) |
| The soldier's sergeant is asleep in the corner of the stable. | (another relevant part of field |
| The soldier is trying to persuade his girl . . . | linguistic role A |
| to run away with him . . . | subject-matter |
| but she wants to know what will happen if they are caught. | linguistic role B |
| They must talk as little as possible so as not to wake the sergeant up. | role of language |

*Figure* 4

The above example helps to show how these variables operate when one is defining a situation for classroom use. It is based on a scene from *Sergeant Musgrave's Dance* by John Arden.

## 6.1.2 The use of definition in practical work

It might very reasonably be objected at this point that introducing the concepts of field, tenor, and mode is only going to complicate a relatively straightforward process. The teacher needs, however, to be able to isolate the variables in a situation in order to extend the possibilities of analytical improvisation. There are three principal ways in which this will help the teacher: it can help him in devising situations to work on; it can enable him and his class to examine changes in linguistic register; it can make possible the exploration of meaning potential and the relationship between situations and the meanings that are possible within them.

### Generating situations

| Tenor | Field | Mode |
|---|---|---|
| A: father/mother B: son/daughter | living room; evening; discussion about pocket money. A watching TV, B doing maths homework | argumentative/persuasive; B seeking to persuade, A seeking to 'block' |
| | living room; late evening (one hour after B has said he/she will be home); A watching TV, B arriving, taking off outdoor clothes; discussion about youth club, where B has just been | imperative/argumentative; A seeking to regulate B's future behaviour, B seeking to explain and persuade |
| | kitchen; breakfast time; A making toast, B doing maths homework; discussion about weekend pop festival some distance away | persuasive; B making request and seeking to persuade, A responding . . . how? |
| | supermarket checkout; two minutes before store closes; A trying to make last minute purchases; B holding basket; discussion about weekend pop festival some distance away | as above |

*Figure 5*

The teacher might, for example, wish to spend a number of lessons exploring the area of parent/child relationships and the subject-matter of teenage responsibility. If he defines tenor simply as 'parent/teenage-child' and then selects a variety of definitions of field and mode he will find that he can then generate a very large number of situations quite easily. The precise tenor will, of course, vary as field and mode change and this in itself provides interesting and worthwhile material for development through improvisation and discussion. The kind of possibilities that open up are illustrated in Figure 5.

**Discussing what behaviour is appropriate**
Secondly, the teacher can work with a class to examine in detail the ways in which different people behave in different situations. He can set up a situation, have the class improvise it, and then, altering only one variable, he can get them to go through the new situation. In the discussion that follows, the class can consider the differences between the two improvisations and the reasons for them.

Suppose, for example, we are looking at requests for help. We might take as a typical situation the dialogue between a customer and a bank manager in the manager's office. This situation with one class of 14-year-olds produced the following:

A  I'm in the grocer's shop round the corner. And my family—my mother and my father and I—have gone into business with the electrical shop down the street and we want an extension on the shop.
B  Mmm
A  So that we can accommodate more utensils, televisons, etcetera—instead of just accessories.
B  Mmm
A  Well, to do this we have to put the sum up, because they've already got the shop.
B  Yes.
A  So we were thinking about trying to get a £6000 extension to the shop.
B  Mmm
A  I was thinking could you—your bank—lend the money?*

The same actors were then asked to work through the same situation, setting it this time in the bar of the local golf club to which the manager and customer both belong.

A . . . Played Charles today.
B Mmm
A Thrashed me. I don't know what was wrong with me.
B Oh?
A I suppose it was the stress. This week it's been telling on me. I've had a lot of worries, the family's been getting at me and . . . . You see we've been trying to get into business with this electrical shop in the town—
B Oh yes?
A And . . . to do that they want us to add an extension to the shop.
B Mmmm?
A And we just haven't been able to raise the money and I can't afford that amount of money anyway, so I've had to sort of go around to people to try to borrow some.
B Well, can't you try the bank?
A What your bank? Of course! I never thought of that.*
(*General laughter from class.*)

In the subsequent discussion with the class, the basic differences between A's two approaches can be considered. In the first scene he is businesslike, as befits the setting, the manager's office. At the club he is more personal, even self-pitying. Attention can then be focused on specific linguistic differences. Why, for example, does the 'electrical shop down the street' become 'this electrical shop in the town'? Why does he change the line from '*we* want an extension on the shop' to '*they want us* to add an extension to the shop'? What changes of tone are taking place? And so on. In all such discussion the role of the teacher is not to point out whether one kind of linguistic behaviour is right or wrong in any particular situation, but to lead pupils towards an awareness of the fact that these differences do occur and what they are like.

It is also possible to construct a series or *chain of situations* in which only one of the variables is changed at a time. The two extracts quoted in this section come from the chain shown in Figure 6. The class can then work through a number of situations in the chain, observing how behaviour alters with each change. Situation chains are also a useful means of moving from situations that children can cope with easily towards those that they may find more difficult because of their complexity or emotional context—a method of gradual stages.

| Tenor | Field | Mode |
|-------|-------|------|
| A: customer<br>B: bank manager<br>(business relationship<br>only) | manager's office; mid-morning; discussion of A's financial problems | explanatory/making request; A seeks loan, B makes relevant professional enquiries |
| as above | golf-club bar; noon; both leaning against bar drinking; discussion of golf and A's financial problems | phatic/merging into professional (explanatory/requesting as above); A seeks loan, B responds |
| A: same person, but defined as club member only<br>B: fellow club member, and friend of A | as above | phatic/personal request; A seeks loan; B responds |
| as above | railway station platform; morning rush-hour; A and B both waiting for train into the city | as above |

Figure 6

## Meaning potential

By manipulating the variables of a situation we can not only examine the differences in linguistic behaviour but we can also begin to understand how it is that meanings which are possible in one situation are not in another.

This can partly be done through the discussion that follows the improvisation, and, in particular, in the third stage of discussion, speculation. The teacher may speculate about the inherent possibilities of a situation in such a way as to make pupils say 'But you couldn't do that' or 'But that's impossible'. The class can then consider what meaning possibilities do or do not exist in any particular situation.

More entertainingly, but just as effectively, 'impossible' or 'totally inappropriate' situations can be set up. In the extract that follows we set out deliberately to disconcert our bank manager. This time the customer who wanted to borrow money was a girl. She came into his room and immediately moved the chair provided for visitors round to the manager's side of his desk and sat down as close to him as she could.

A Well, how are we today?

B (*very nervous and taken aback*). Oh . . . all right. And what can I do for you?

A (*expansively*)—Well, I was wondering—you know if you could lend us some money. Some dough—you know.

B What's this money for?

A Oh, just to spend—yeah.

B Well, we don't really sort of lend out money just to spend.

A (*airily*). I always thought you had money just to spend.

B It has to be—you know—on a certain thing.

A The lady down the road did.

B Yes, well, she must have borrowed some money for a certain thing.

A Well, so she says but she hasn't spent it on a certain thing. She came in here wanting to buy a horse. A horse my foot! . . . Well, I was hoping you could lend me . . . £600.

B 600? Just so that you can go out and spend it?

A Well, I need some new clothes, don't I?

B Well, we don't exactly lend it out just like that for clothes. It's for property, or . . . .

A What you mean property?

B A house or—

A I want a house. Can you lend me £600?*

In discussions about language, tape recorders can be used to isolate speech and remove the 'distraction' of gesture, facial expression, and so on. For example, a pair of pupils may be given a recorder and a short period of time in which to record two situations, changing only one variable. The recording is then played back to the rest of the class who have to try to work out from what they hear the differences between the two recordings and the reasons for them.

## 6.2 Paralanguage

As has already been suggested (1.1.2), we are seriously limiting ourselves if we restrict our work on situations to linguistic features only. Paralanguage, kinesics, and proxemics are also of fundamental importance to the meanings we can make and take in any situation. Some of these features we are aware of in everyday life, and comment on, while others affect us only unconsciously. Yet they do affect us, and it is

74

valuable to draw attention to some or all of them. (The sensory skills involved in picking up paralinguistic signals are obviously very important in everyday life as well as in classroom improvisation.)

First the teacher must draw out what the observers have actually seen in as much detail as possible (see 5.3.1). Even in this there will be considerable disagreement because of the subtle interplay of observation and interpretation in the mind. The following questions about different aspects of paralinguistic behaviour might help to clarify observation.

1 Direction of gaze
Did the other person look you in the eye? For what proportion of the total time? For what period of time in each case? How much did his eyes move around? In how many different directions did he look?

2 Facial expression
What emotions did his eyes and mouth suggest during the interaction? What did they suggest about his attitude towards the general subject matter of the dialogue? Towards the other participants? What specific comment did they suggest on details of the speech of the others? Did they provide a gloss on details of his own speech? Were eyes and mouth 'in agreement' about the emotion or attitudes they expressed? Or did he smile with his mouth and not with his eyes?

3 Vocal effects
How did the speaker's vocal delivery affect the surface meaning of what he had to say? How as his meaning affected by his speed and rhythm of speech, by pauses silent and vocalized ('er' and 'um'), by intonation? As a result was there ambiguity? Was there a counterpoint, or even a direct contradiction between surface meaning and real intention?

4 Gesture
How frequent and vigorous were the participants' gestures? Was this constant or was there a variety? How did they relate to the subject matter and emotional context of the situation? How did the physical qualities of gesture and the vocal qualities of speech relate?

5 Posture
Were the participants sitting or standing? Inclined towards, or away from each other? Was the line of the body straight or flexed? Were both feet supporting the weight of the body or only one? Was any other part of the body taking weight? What was the position of hands and arms when at rest?

## 6 Relative positioning

How close to each other were the participants? Did both seek to maintain this degree of proximity or did one seek to alter it? Were both
maintaining a similar posture or was there a difference? Did one seek to
use their relative positioning to alter the situation, by achieving physical
dominance, for example?

He can then bring the pupils to make explicit the conclusions they
have drawn from their observations. There is, of course, no 'right'
answer, nor any particular need for agreement about what any paralinguistic signals mean. The aim is rather to establish that we are affected by these features, what they are, and how different individuals
interpret them. The teacher's function is to concentrate the attention
of the class on the fact that there is evidence (what they see and hear)
and there are deductions: in other words, to make explicit what is often
vague and impressionistic.

### 6.2.1 The paralanguage exercise

There is an exercise that can profitably be used specifically to draw
attention to paralanguage.

The pupils in pairs or small groups are given a short script extract
which they learn. This is deliberately ambiguous, so that different
groups can each interpret it in a number of ways. Characters are not
referred to by name, only by letter:

A  I only go there to get some fresh air
B  Exactly
A  Exactly what
B  Exactly that
A  Why shouldn't I go there to get some fresh air

The groups then discuss the kind of situation of which these lines might
form a part. (Or they may be asked to devise more than one situation.)
Having decided on a situation, they improvise the whole interaction,
using the script lines at some point in their scene. They then discuss
how the situation causes them to interpret the lines, both vocally and
physically, and they practise the extract on its own to ensure that they
can repeat their own interpretation exactly.

Each group then performs the extract to the rest. It is generally useful to have a group do each extract twice, because the extracts are so brief (see Appendix on the use of closed circuit television here). The rest of the class are then asked a number of questions about the relationship and the situation to which the extract may belong, in order to point out the paralinguistic elements that they should be aware of. The answers may be written (if the teacher wants a genuine comparison of the impressions of the whole class), or for discussion. The questions can include the following:

1 Character
Is A relaxed or tense?
Is she confident?
Is she sincere?
2 Relationship
Does A know B well or are they strangers?
Does A trust B?
Does she respect him?
Does she like him?
Does she believe him?
3 Situation
Who is on their 'home ground' here?
Who is trying to dominate the exchange?
Who is attacking and who is defending?
In general what do you think the situation is?

The questioning proceeds from what is specific and relatively easily perceived to that which is more general and needs more reflection. It is, of course, extremely difficult to answer these questions on such flimsy evidence, although the knowledge that questions will be asked will help to sharpen both the interpretation of those performing and the perception of those watching. (This knowledge should not be allowed to lead the performers to indulge in caricature or burlesque, however). In the second stage of discussion the performers explain what they are trying to do. They may need to go through the improvised situation which they used in their preparation.

## 6.2.2 Other practical work

It can frequently be useful to focus on paralinguistic behaviour when building up an improvised situation. In working out a character, for example, one can take as a starting point a habitual gesture, or a typical facial expression or posture, and investigate how much this can tell us about the whole character. Similarly a relationship can be developed from a typical relative positioning of two characters. However, sometimes it is useful to work directly on paralanguage, without relating it to speech. Realistic situations which do not involve speech are difficult to devise, as extralinguistic behaviour usually supports linguistic, but mime and dramatic movement are two activities that concentrate attention on the relationship between physical behaviour and meaning.

The word 'mime' is here used to mean any acting without words in which meaning is expressed according to certain conventions. These may be traditional, as in the case of classical mime, or specific to one medium, as in the silent films, or established by actors for the purposes of a particular piece of work. Pupils may be set to tell a story, express a situation, or simply demonstrate an activity, in such a way that movement, gesture, and facial expression convey all the meaning that is necessary. The emphasis here is on expression to others, rather than imagining or experiencing, because it is from the difficulites of expressing meaning without the use of language that the value of the exercise derives.

Dramatic movement, however, focuses more on imagining and experiencing than on expression. Often such work starts from a stimulus such as a piece of music, a theme, or an emotion, and is built up in terms that are personal to the individual or group involved. The expression of meaning is very much a secondary consideration. Here too it is interesting and worthwhile to examine the degree to which a piece of movement draws on the conventions of everyday life or of earlier art to convey meaning, and how much an individual or group establishes a new 'language' specific to the piece of work.

## 6.3 Presentation of self

So far in this chapter we have concentrated first on the observation of behaviour and secondly on the deductions that can be made from it. However, this is not necessarily the order in which human beings approach an interaction in everyday life. It is almost impossible to enter an interaction with a mind free from preconceptions, and one's observation is rarely, if ever, unaffected by one's attitudes. The American sociologist, Erving Goffman (1955) writes:

Every person lives in a world of social encounters, involving him either in face-to-face or mediated contact with other participants. In each of these contacts, he tends to act out what is sometimes called a *line*—that is, a pattern of verbal and non-verbal acts by which he expresses his view of the situation and through this his evaluation of the participants, particularly himself.

Our own perception of the constraints of the situation makes us aware of its meaning possibilities, which we can then exploit in the appropriate linguistic behaviour.

As Goffman points out, however, people do not necessarily perceive situations in the same way. Since each participant in an interaction will seek to project his own definiton of the situation, there must be an element of co-operation between participants for an interaction to progress. Goffman (1959) describes this as follows:

When we allow that the individual projects a definition of the situation when he appears before others, we must also see that the others, however passive their role may seem to be, will themselves effectively project a definition of the situation by virtue of their response to the individual and by virtue of any lines of action they initiate to him. Ordinarily the definitions of the situation projected by the several different participants are sufficiently attuned to one another, so that open contradiction will not occur. . . . The maintenance of this surface of agreement, this veneer of consensus, is facilitated by each participant concealing his own wants behind statements which assert values to which everyone present feels obliged to give lip service . . . . We then have a kind of interactional *modus vivendi*.

If we cannot agree on the interpretation of the situation, or if, for some reason, the *modus vivendi* breaks down, then the interaction can lead to embarrassment or even open conflict.

Goffman's observations make clear a major difference between the types of co-operation involved in a dramatic situation and in the real life situation. Normally improvisation is seen by teachers as a highly co-operative activity. A group of students is given a certain amount of information or the students decide it for themselves before they begin, and then they act out the situation. All of the group share all the information, and may even co-operate to the extent of discussing in general terms how the scene should go. Such sharing does not, of course, occur in real life. Some information about the situation may be common to all those involved, but much of it is personal, since it is based on individual interpretation and is therefore inferential. We observe the behaviour of others, interpret it for our own benefit and act accordingly. Goffman suggests that the signs which we give off to the others involved in an interaction are intended to indicate to them the way in which we think the scene should be structured and normally after a preliminary period we find we are able to agree on an interpretation that takes account of this and we can then proceed with a high degree of co-operation. This co-operation, however, clearly differs from that used in the 'prepared' improvisation, since it only takes place implicitly and after there has been a fairly complex kind of guessing game. The co-operation involved in improvisation allows few opportunities for this kind of 'guessing', if any at all. There is little or no uncertainty in the interpretation of the situation or the roles. To provide greater realism, therefore, it is useful to set up situations in which all the information about a scene, or about the characters in it, is *not* shared by all the actors. In this way it is possible to achieve a greater approximation to what actually happens in interactions and also to allow students to see more clearly the kind of co-operation that takes place in real life between participants as an interaction unfolds.

### 6.3.1 Providing special information

**One out of the group**
The simplest procedure is to provide only one person with special information. An example will illustrate this. The teacher tells the group of four:

This is set in an insurance office and there are four characters. There's the manager, Mr. Waylett, the senior clerk, Miss Clarke, a shorthand typist, Anne Richards, and a junior clerk who does all the odd jobs. So far it's been a happy office with a rather easy-going boss. It's the end of the coffee break and Miss Clarke is just going round trying to sort out the holiday roster. Right? Mr. Waylett, come over here and the rest of you sort out the furniture for the office and then get started.

The pupil playing Mr. Waylett is then given further instructions orally, but so that the others can't hear them:

You've received a letter from Head Office to say that your office is inefficient and over-staffed. You have been told that you will have to get rid of one of your junior employees. Decide how you're going to do it and then get started.


## Intervention

Another method is to brief an extra actor while an improvisation is actually going on. Once the scene outlined above had started, the teacher might give another actor the following instruction:

You are Anne Richard's boy friend. You occasionally call in at the office to meet her. Today you want to see her to arrange a date for the evening. Right—start now.

Alternatively, the teacher can himself be the intervening actor. This has the advantage that the teacher will be able to control the improvisation to some extent and will also be able to help the other actors if they are momentarily thrown by the intervention. Intervention serves two purposes: it increases the chance of spontaneity as well as providing plenty of opportunity for the observation of the different lines taken and the way in which they shift as the situation alters.


## The group application

In order to approximate more closely to real life interaction in which every participant has his own line, every member of an improvisation group needs to have separate instructions. The most practical way in which to do this is to prepare worksheets for the actors. Each actor receives two sets of instructions—one of information shared by the whole group and the other which is special to him. This technique is illustrated fully in 9.2.2. The unexpectedness engendered by this method will normally pay off the extra preparation required.

Special information can be used in a number of ways: groups of pupils preparing their own ideas for improvisation may well allow time for individual private thought and preparation immediately before the improvisation begins; the teacher can prepare large scale work by means of a set of cards of character and situation information which can be distributed according to the particular needs of a group within a project. Thus improvisation work which is analytical or exploratory can be synthesized into large-scale projects which could be for ultimate performance of some kind.

## 6.3.2 Setting up conflicting interpretations

The practical applications of Goffman's analysis may be taken one stage further. The teacher can deliberately set up situations which two characters, or two groups of characters, interpret in radically different ways, and in which each seeks to impose his definition on the other. Again the two characters or groups are instructed separately either orally or by means of a worksheet. The following examples suggest the kind of situations that allow of this kind of work.

1  A local council meeting at which the report of the finance and general purposes committee is to be approved. It is an open meeting and a local environmentalist lobby is there in force to set up a protest about some local problem. The council members are primed with their own political pre-occupations so that they don't see this coming.

2  Interview between boss and young employee. Employee thinks firm is easy-going and welcoming and has idea for saving money and time in one of the processes. Boss has come to think of employee as young upstart and wants to give him a dressing-down.

3  Meeting between boyfriend and girlfriend. Boy has secretly planned holiday for the two of them with a crowd of friends that summer and wants to discuss it. Girl has decided that she wants to leave the area (and therefore boy) and take exciting job abroad. She is looking for an opportunity to break this to boyfriend.

# 7
# Improvisation and synthesis

When I think about any interaction I have been involved in, I can consider it in two different ways: I may look at its individual components, or I may try to see it in some kind of broader context. In the previous chapter we looked at the different components that make up individual interaction, and considered how these could be used to build up or to break down an improvised dramatic scene. This is not only a linguistically valid way of treating the matter, it also parallels the common sense way in which people tend to view interactions. People do think about their meetings with others and attempt to analyse the way in which they have behaved, the words that were used and so on. They do not do this for every encounter, however, and some people rarely if ever consider their lives in this way. More frequently, we listen to 'what goes on inside our head' (see 1.2.2) and are aware of the personal continuity between the different roles we play and the situations in which we play them. When observing others, too, we relate the behaviour of a particular person or persons to what we knew of them before and to our own experience of how people in general have tended to behave in such situations in the past. Moreover, using this experience we may speculate about possible future situations. In this way we seek to contextualize our own and other people's behaviour. As Halliday (1974a) points out:

. . . language is the medium through which a human being becomes a personality, in consequence of his membership of society and his occupancy of social roles.

This concept of personal and social context provides a second important area for improvised dramatic work with adolescents. The last chapter showed how the basic improvised situation of Chapters 4 and 5 can be used to analyse what happens in one particular interaction. This chapter will consider how we may place the interaction in its context in the life of the individual or individuals involved, and how the inner life of the individual, and of the relationships and groups in which he participates, provides a synthesis of the separate features of situations discussed before.

## 7.1 Individuals

The simplest beginning to seeing an interaction in some context is to consider the central character of a single scene. We ask what he did before and after that scene (just as, from time to time in the theatre one asks oneself much the same question about the characters in a play). Ideas about other relationships or groups he is involved in may also be useful. We can then begin to see that situation as one of a historical sequence concerning that character. The sequence may concern one period or one issue in his life, or it may examine several important events.

There are two main methods for working on series of situations that are linked by one central character:

1 The character is undefined, and gradually emerges through the decisions that the actor takes 'on behalf of' the character.
2 The character is verbally defined to start off with and then characteristic traits and qualities are embodied in action.

### 7.1.1 Development through action

When the character is developed through action, the central principle is a simple one. After any situation has been worked on the teacher may simply say: 'What would happen if we took that character and put him in a situation where . . .' or 'How would that character behave if . . .?' When the character is left verbally undefined in this way, the participants in a situation are free to use or reject elements from their own experience as they wish. The definiton of character is thus done purely in action as situation succeeds situation. In each situation, predicament, or escapade the actor thus has to make choices of behaviour that are consistent with what has gone before. Both in discussion and in the way the situations are inter-related the pressure is put on the actors to maintain this consistency. The choices that are made in the various situations thus gradually define a character who has internal consistency and is to some degree separate from the actor.[1]

The kinds of situations that are chosen will depend largely on the age of the pupils. Younger pupils will enjoy a picaresque format, in which situations are based on adventures and scrapes which make life—and personal consistency—more and more difficult for the central character. While this work may be of interest for older adolescents as well, they will increasingly want to incorporate accurate social detail into the sequence of situations. Scenes in which the central character is forced to compare himself with others, or in which he has role-playing problems will parallel the kind of difficulties that the actors themselves are facing in real life. Thus we may move from practical jokes, apple stealing, and pocket money problems to staying out late at night, holidays a long way from home, and boyfriend trouble. Equally the work may develop away from direct social realism of this type towards situations from literature that put a central character under various kinds of personal stress (for example, Arnold Haithwaite in John Rowe Townsend's *The Intruder*, Pip in Dickens' *Great Expectations* or Nicky Gore in *The Devil's Children* by Peter Dickinson).

### 7.1.2 Working from a definition

In the second method the emphasis is on the definiton of the central character in words and the interest lies in the way in which these concepts and qualities are embodied in action. The opening definition can be as simple as the instruction, 'The Captain (from the *Commedia dell'Arte* stories) always boasts how brave he is, but really he's a coward', or as complex as, 'Falstaff's attitude to courage is summed up in his speech:

Well, 'tis no matter, honour pricks me on. Yea, but how if honour prick me off when I come on, how then? Can honour set to a leg? No. (*Henry IV,* Part 1, V.i)

In either case, by asking an actor to base his character's behaviour on the words we have given him, we are asking him to test his own ideas, in this case about different types of cowardice, by putting them into an active form. Different children will have different interpretations of qualities such as courage, cowardice, truth, deception, and so on. These differences will be highlighted in the situation and can then be discussed.

As well as being based on specific characters such as these, work may focus on more idealized or heroic characters. With children and adolescents the ideal self[2] is often strongly influenced by the folk heroes who exist in their sub-culture, derived from a number of sources, including the mass media and local and popular tradition. These archetypal figures and the situations in which they occur affect the development of many ideals still adhered to much later in life, and ideas of right and wrong in general. The characters, and the qualities and conflicts they embody, are central to the play of younger children which is strongly traditional in many of its forms. These forms, such as cowboys and Indians, cops and robbers, can last actively into secondary education and the memory of them certainly does. So the teacher can look either to this traditional 'hall of fame' or to the richer and more complex heroes and heroines from mythology and literature for archetypal figures on which to base improvisation. Working from these, the children may choose to project their own ideal self, or explore a wide variety of abstract qualities and concepts.

### 7.1.3 An example

The two methods of working on a single character represent two extremes, between which there is a full range of possible combinations of elements of the two approaches. The scene that follows, by third year pupils, comes from a sequence of scenes about a girl who has a dream self whom she sees when she gazes into her mirror, and the contrast between her dream life and reality. (The dream self was in fact played by another actress, and the whole sequence devised for work on closed circuit television.) In this scene Darrel has just been dreaming, when the telephone in her room rings.

(*Darrel is sitting at her dressing table, on which there is a large mirror. She is gazing into the mirror, when the phone rings. She picks it up.*)
DARREL  Hullo . . . yes? . . . Russell? Russell who? . . . Well I . . . I don't remember . . . Oh-oh yes, yes, I know . . . Eh? . . . When? . . . me? . . . Oh um, I'd like to, but—. . . coffee? . . . all right then, what time? . . . seven? . . . Yes-yes I'm sure. I will come, I will . . . promise . . . All right then, seven o'clock . . . OK. Bye.

(*She puts the phone down and looks at the mirror. Half thoughtful and half smiling, she holds her hair up behind her head, creating a new hairstyle for herself. The door opens and her Father comes in and crosses the room to sit down near her. She lets her hair go, and turns to face him; then she looks back at the mirror.*)

FATHER  Who was that?

DARREL  Russell.

FATHER  Russell who?

(*Pause.*)

DARREL  (*looking down*). Howard.

FATHER  Who's he? . . . Who's he?

DARREL  A boy.

FATHER  (*smiling ironically, but maintaining an even tone*). No, who?

DARREL  Russell Howard.

FATHER  (*patient, but firm*). Darrel, you know what I mean. Where did you meet him, who is he?

DARREL  He said I met him at a party.

(*Pause.*)

FATHER  Do you remember?

(*Slightly longer pause. Darrel turns to face him.*)

DARREL  I *think* I do.

FATHER  You *think* so . . . what did he want?

(*Short pause. Darrel turns slowly to face him.*)

DARREL  To take me out.

FATHER  Where?

DARREL  The pictures.

FATHER  (*remaining calm, but his tone betraying a deep suspicion of the whole business*). You *think* you remember him.

DARREL  I'm *sure* I remember him.

(*Long pause and then she turns to face him.*) Can I go? . . . I mean I want to go . . . . (*She turns back to mirror.*) . . . and if I do my hair . . . (*She tries the new hair style in the mirror.*)

FATHER  What's happened to Gary now? It soon wore off, didn't it?

DARREL  He wasn't nice and I don't think he found me nice anyway.

FATHER  How do you know that Russell will?

DARREL  He told me I'd got strawy hair—and I haven't. (*Looks at it in mirror.*)

FATHER  (*getting a little exasperated*). Well, Russell might say that!

DARREL  . . . (*Words indistinguishable on tape.*) . . . if he wanted to take me out.

FATHER  Gary wanted to take you out.

DARREL  It's nice to have someone like him. (*Turns back to father.*) Can I go, Dad? It'll be really my first . . . my first . . . big date. I mean with Gary I just went to watch him play football and I felt really stupid.

FATHER  It seems a bit silly to go with someone you don't even know if you've met him . . . . (*He is allowing him to be persuaded.*)

DARREL  I'm sure I've met him . . . and I'll bring him home to meet·you. He's going to meet me outside the pictures at seven o'clock tomorrow.

FATHER  Well, I don't suppose I can do much. It's up to you, I suppose.

DARREL  (*Big smile.*) Thanks Dad. (*She turns back to the mirror and tries out that hairstyle again.*)*

There was nothing extraordinary about the scene, but the girl was able to see—and show—not only herself with her father, but also an inner world in which she was dreaming about her 'first big date', how she would look, how the boy would behave, and how totally different it was all going to be from her relationship with Gary. The way in which the mirror was used, and the strategic use of pauses helped to create a very 'quiet' scene in which no great overt emotion was expressed but which nevertheless had an intensity that struck the other members of the class with the force of reality.

## 7.2 Pairs

Another way of setting a single situation in its context is to follow procedures similar to those that have just been described, but to concentrate attention on a relationship between two people rather than on a single central character. This may lead naturally to the realization that relationships do not take place in a vacuum. In the scene about pocket money quoted in 5.2, for example, we may feel that much of the conversation is unreal, because no relationship between father and son has been realized. It would be useful in this case to work on other scenes between father and son with different subject matter, different problems, so that the relationship and their roles within it can be more clearly defined.

When working on relationships, it is useful to have some simple frames of reference, both when planning work and when leading discussions. For present purposes, three can be outlined: role-relationship; self-disclosure; and team-work. In any relationship, first of all, there is a period during which areas to be included within the relationship are defined, when the two participants decide, as it were, what the relationship is 'about'. Thus I may develop a fairly cordial relationship with a colleague for purely professional purposes, but as we discover 'how much we have in common' that relationship may well develop into something that is far more important and 'personal' to both participants than the professional relationship from which it arose.

Then, as the relationship progresses and mutual 'trust' develops, the amount of self-disclosure[3] may be expected to increase. This amount— and the nature of what is disclosed—will in turn help to determine the nature of the relationship that develops. The view that the two participants in the relationship have of what is 'proper' within it will determine the kind of information they consider it appropriate to disclose and the language in which it should be couched. One may discuss one's sex life with one's analyst and also with a friend from the rugger club, but the language is likely to be different.

Finally, as the relationship becomes more established, the pair can increasingly be expected to operate as a team when in the presence of other people, and particularly when they feel that the relationship itself is threatened. If someone accuses my wife of petty theft I am more likely to stand by her (and disbelieve the accuser) and if the same accusation is made, for example, against a professional colleague.

For adolescents, the question of defining relationships is very important and many of them find improvisation work concentrating on this area particularly interesting and rewarding. How far does a particular relationship go? What is it 'about'? Who is responsible for what within it? These problems can usefully be explored by the device of subjecting an existing relationship to some kind of serious test. The relationship that is used may be one from another situation that has already been developed, or it may be set up specifically for the purpose. The teacher then devises some threat that will call the whole relationship into question. The threat can be external—most obviously, some kind of open interference. 'You must stop seeing this boy', for example. An external threat puts pressure on the participants in the relationship to determine not only its nature but also its strength. Is this the 'real thing', or just another boy/girl relationship? Do both agree about that? If it is, how do they cope with parents? Fight? Agree to meet in secret? Separate for a while? Who decides this, organizes it? And so on. A more subtle threat comes from inside the relationship—perhaps when disagreement arises about the true nature of the relationship (one of two 'good friends' starts looking in jewellers' windows, for example).

Often external and internal threats coincide, as in the following example. The group was given as a starting point an extract from *A Kind of Loving* by Stan Barstow. It begins

'Hello,' she says. 'I've brought my friend along. I hope you don't mind.' 'Oh, no . . . no,' I say like a clot. But what else can I say for Pete's sake? My heat's dropped down into my boots with a thud because I know straight my number's up. This is one way of doing it, giving you the shove . . . .

The passage (Penguin edition, pp. 65–71) is too long to quote in full, but the gist of it is that Vic, the narrator, and Ingrid's friend Dorothy have a row about Vic's past and his resentment both at her presence there at all, and at the way in which she is behaving. Vic reduces Dorothy to tears and Ingrid has to hurry after her to calm her down.

INGRID  Hullo, Vic.
VIC  Hullo . . . where'd you like to go tonight?
INGRID  I thought we'd go to the pictures.
VIC  OK, I thought we'd go there. I thought we'd see *Love Story* or *Fist of Fury*.
DOROTHY  I don't wanna see no *Fist of Fury*.
INGRID  By the way this is Dorothy. Dorothy–Vic.
DOROTHY  How do you do, Vic. Hey! . . . hey, I know you. He used to chase me and Angela along the river bank. I know Vic all right, don't I, Vic. (*She laughs.*) Oh dear, if only you could have been there . . . never mind.
INGRID  Yeah, well, come on, the pictures.
DOROTHY  Oh, it doesn't start for another fifteen minutes . . . .
VIC  It starts in five minutes.
DOROTHY  Oh Vic, didn't you used to go to my school?
VIC  No.
DOROTHY  (*whispering to Ingrid, from which we hear only the name 'Paul' and the final words*) . . . and cross my heart and hope to die he said she liked him. Honestly . . . honestly he did. Oh I nearly dropped dead . . . .
VIC  You're just trying to stir up trouble, aren't you? You're just trying to stir up trouble between Ingrid and me.
DOROTHY  Who do you thing you're talking to, '*boy*'?
VIC  I'm talking to you, '*girl*'.

DOROTHY  Oh shut up!

VIC  You're just trying to stir up trouble saying about that Paul.

DOROTHY  Oh—

VIC  There's no such Paul.

(*Confused talk undecipherable on tape.*)

VIC  I wouldn't lay a finger on you.

DOROTHY  I wouldn't look at you.

VIC  I wouldn't lay a finger on you.

(*More confused talk.*)

DOROTHY  It's none of your business, or don't you remember?

VIC  I could just slap that grin right across your face.

DOROTHY  You touch me, boy, and I'll give you one back.

VIC  Yes, You just watch it.

DOROTHY  Oh shut your face.

INGRID  Oh come on, let's go to the pictures.

DOROTHY  Oh some friend you are, walking off with him. Go on—go on. (*She leaves them, nearly in tears.*)

INGRID  Now see what you've done.

VIC  I don't care about her—I don't know why you're friends with her.

INGRID  She's my best friend, well, I—

VIC  I don't care if she's your best friend. I'm not going to the pictures with her.

INGRID  Well, I'm going. (*She follows Dorothy, leaving Vic alone.*)*

## 7.3 Groups

### 7.3.1 Four types of group

Different types of group can be used in a variety of ways to place an interaction in context. The most obvious groups for present purposes are family, work, adolescent, and problem-solving groups.

For nearly everyone, *the family* is the fundamental context, for much of our thinking, and talking, about ourselves and our most intimate personal relationships. The actual families of those taking part can be used as a starting point, or imaginary, different family organizations may be relevant. ('We have seen how your families deal with this problem; now what would happen if we had a family organization where everyone had a second, artificial family to whom they could go when they had fallen out with their real family, as in Aldous Huxley's *Island*?') *Work groups*, which again many people are closely involved in later in life, can also be based on probable future occupations of pupils, or on more exotic professions (professional footballers, or popstars, for example).

Argyle (1969) says of *adolescent groups*:

During adolescence work and family attachments are weak and the strongest attachments are to friends. These groups are formed of young people between the ages of 11/12 up to 21/23, when the members marry and settle down in jobs, and other kinds of group become more important to them. The motivations of members are partly to engage in various joint activities but more important are interpersonal needs— sexual, affiliative, and the establishment of identity . . . . Conversation is mainly about other adolescents, parents, interpersonal feelings, and social interaction.

Such groups are the most strongly felt and most likely to be criticized or undervalued by adults. Improvised drama can redress the balance by putting them in their rightful central place, but within a working setting that does not allow their discussion to degenerate into sentimental maunderings.[4]

Finally, the improvisation group itself is a *problem-solving group*—a group which has come together on one occasion, or does so regularly, with specific tasks to fulfil. Planning groups and committees of various kinds are typical of this category, and so are international sports touring sides, or teams of spies and saboteurs. Many such groups are by definition *ad hoc* and quite often short-lived. Role relationships, patterns of dominance/submission, and degrees of mutual trust have to be worked out quickly and often in terms that are fairly stark. Moreover, the participants often have little prior information on which to base their judgements, which thus have to be made 'on the job'. Such problem-solving groups can coincide with what might be called 'accidental' groups which drama teachers often invent for improvisation purposes: plane crashes, shipwrecks, car accidents, and so on all have the advantage that they bring together a range of ill-assorted characters who might not normally be expected to associate. In addition there is usually that 'element of desperation'[5] in the group's struggle to survive, which is likely to stimulate improvisation.

### 7.3.2 The situation and the group

One of the ways in which a single situation can be developed further is by setting the situation in a group context. If we are working on a scene in which one boy accuses another of taking something from his desk, one way of examining the issues involved is to translate this situation to the broader context of the adolescent group of friends to which both belong and where it is often easier to establish the moral values involved in this particular conflict.

Alternatively, a series of situations can be shaped by taking a central character through the different groups of which he is a member. As Argyle points out (1969), one of the problems adolescents have to cope with is that they have 'to come to terms with the difficulty of playing different roles on different occasions'. So if we take one central character and give him a specific problem to deal with—whether it is being caught stealing apples, or coming to terms with the fact that his widowed mother intends to remarry—we can then get him to carry this particular burden to the various groups of which he is a member. He finds that not only must be present his problem in different ways, but he also has to present himself differently. If the problem is one that is felt to be serious, the central character's behaviour thus raises the whole question of the relationship between sincerity of attitude and variety of self-presentation. A pair relationship can also be moved from group to group so that we see it in the context of the different groups of which the two people involved are members.

The group can, of course, be ready-made the teacher asks the class to form groups of the required number and type, and then allows the ethos and authority structure[6] of the particular group—whether it is family, work, or whatever—to emerge during the initial improvisation. If the teacher wishes to have more control, however, and to determine in advance what the group is going to be like, this can be done by gradually building the group up, starting with pair work, and then adding two pairs together to make a four, and so on. By specifying the pair situation fairly carefully, the attitudes of the whole group are gradually determined in the course of the preparatory work (and, of course, the characters are worked out at the same time). Such a process is particularly useful with children who have little experience either of drama or of group work.

## 7.4 Planning the lesson

The various contexts discussed in this chapter will provide a variety of ways of organizing material either in the single lesson or in a sequence of lessons. Although the pattern of work will depend finally on the decision of the individual teacher, it might be useful to look at two extremes of planning, to get some idea of the range of possibilities.

### 7.4.1. Detailed pre-planning

If the teacher wishes to plan everything very carefully before he begins, the contexts of character, pair relationship, and group provide some 'skeleton' plans along the following lines:

1 Central character
a taken through, and defined by, selected situations;
b as hero defined by qualities and traits;
c seen in a series of significant relationships, not necessarily historical or related;
d seen as a member of different groups.
2 Central relationship
a viewed historically and defined in selected situations;
b established and then tested by external or internal threats;
c seen in terms of complementary or conflicting group membership of the two participants
3 Central group
a gradually built up of its constituent parts, developing ethos and role structure;
b *vis-à-vis* one member;
c *vis-à-vis* other groups to which its members belong;
d its reaction to situations and problems that affect it as a group.

### 7.4.2 'Wait and see'

Alternatively, the teacher may 'wait and see' what develops in the lesson. One often hears drama teachers emphasizing that they need to be very flexible, to be ready to scrap what has been prepared and strike out on an entirely new track if the lesson demands it. But the prospect may seem daunting for the inexperienced teacher who does not, perhaps, have much confidence in his own ability to abandon carefully-made plans and perhaps extemporize nearly the whole of a lesson. He needs some theoretical framework in which this possibility may be set. Again, the context of the single character, the pair relationship, or the group will provide a number of lines of development from the improvisation of one situation. Some of the questions we can ask to pursue any of these lines are:

1 Concerning any individual
a How does his behaviour towards individual A fit into the general pattern of their relationship?
b How does his behaviour towards the rest of the group fit into the general pattern of his relationship with the group?
c Is he maintaining a consistent self-image? Can we take him out of this scene, put him in another situation, and believe in him as a real person?
d What about the way he presents himself? How would this person present himself, what role would be assume in another situation?
2 Concerning any pair relationship
a What happens when we take two out of this scene and isolate them (leave them alone together)?
b What happens when we take them out of this context and put them in a different group situation?
c What is the history of this relationship?
d How do the pair define this relationship and what would happen if it were tested by some internal or external threat?
3 Concerning the whole group
a What is the history, structure, ethos of this group?
b In what ways can the group be subdivided?
c How do its members behave in the other groups of which they are members?

These are only some of the questions that can be asked about any situation, and each question can lead to many further situations. Each of these can lead to further questions, and so on.

### 7.4.3 The group, the class, and the teacher

In Chapter 5 both group- and class-work had clear functions. The work described in this chapter obviously demands a more flexible approach. Much of the time the emphasis will be on group work. There are, however, still occasions when the teacher will find it useful to draw the attention of the whole class to the work of one particular group:

1  As a focus for discussion, whether by separate groups, or by the class as a whole.
2  Because of some special values or problems it contains.
3  As a fresh starting point: the teacher may decide to take the work of one group as a focus for discussion and then develop from it a series of situations for all groups to work on.
4  As preparation for a larger performance project (see next chapter).

Nevertheless, in work that emphasizes the personal or interpersonal context of any interaction, much of the time the teacher's role is that of adviser, questioner, or one-man audience, as he moves from group to group while the work is in progress. Indeed, once the lesson has been started, he may find that the does not address the class as a whole again until the end of the lesson.

## 7.5 Discussion

When one is working on the interpersonal context within which individual interactions are set, group and class discussion are clearly very important. The significance—and difficulties—of such discussion are underlined by Creber (1972).

Experience alone is not enough, for we hardly possess it until it is articulated. For this to happen, the pupil needs to feel comfortable in a way rarely possible in a formal classroom where the presence of the teacher, to say nothing of thirty-five other pupils, imposes social constraints which inhibit precisely the kinds of talk that are needed . . . . It is significant that thinking aloud is an activity not normally encouraged by the speech climate in the classroom. This is particularly true at secondary level where teachers may be so preoccupied with their own conception of what is to be learnt that they ignore or actively discourage other kinds of learning; there is not time to wait while pupils *grope their way towards thought.*

And he continues

It is probably only in the pupil-to-pupil talk of small groups that the adolescent can feel safe enough to think aloud in a way that enables him to 'realize' and recognize aspects of his experience, his emotions, his personality that he has hitherto kept private even from himself.

These needs have been recognized in curriculum developments such as the Nuffield humanities scheme. Such projects usually take as a stimulus some form of fairly passive experience by the group—a TV programme, film, or tape, or the shared reading of a piece of source material. The following discussion is in terms of the past experience of the members of the group and includes their opinions about that experience and about the starting material. What drama does is to impose an activity. Source material may still be used and the activity will usually be followed by discussion about personal experience and opinion. In between, however, the group is set a practical problem which itself involves the disclosure and articulation of personal experience. If I am a member of a group preparing and then performing an improvisation about an imaginary family, then I cannot avoid some reference to my own experience of family both in the pre-performance discussion and in my performance as an actor. This process has the advantage of being distanced. 'Officially' I am talking about how families in general behave or how a particular imaginary family does, not necessarily about how my own family behaves. It is also never clear to the other members of the group—or to the audience, if there is one—just how much of my own experience I am actually using when I act, and I know that it is not clear. The use of improvisation, therefore—once one has overcome the initial difficulties of the activity itself (see Chapter 3)—can be a most liberating technique for many adolescents in the articulation of their own private experience.

   Most of the time the discussion will be in the same small groups in which the improvisation has taken place. This raises the problem of how the teacher should organize work so that the discussions may be as relevant and useful as possible. In the work described in Chapters 5 and 6, this was done through teacher-led class discussion: now it must be done by the way in which the lesson units themselves are structured. The pattern for a lesson unit developed in Chapter 5 was:

preliminary work → performance → discussion

This pattern remains, but the preliminary work is largely composed of preparatory discussion by the group. The teacher thus has two chances of shaping the discussion that takes place: first by the starting point he gives for the improvisation; and secondly by any specific instructions he gives about what the group should be looking for in the discussion that follows it.

## 7.5.1 Before the improvisation

The discussion leading up to the improvisation can be shaped by the amount and nature of detailed information given to the group by the teacher. Whether this is done through his own explanation, through written material, or a combination of the two, the less detail that is given the freer and broader we may expect the discussion to be and vice versa. An example will make this clear. The subject is boyfriends and the context the family. The instruction may simply be: 'Work out an improvised scene about a family row about boyfriends.' In this case the range of preliminary discussion could be very wide. One member of the group might recount her own experience, perhaps leading to a general swapping of experiences before the scene itself is planned at all.

If, however, the teacher wants to concentrate attention on one specific area of the problem, he will give plenty of detail about the parts of the scene he does not particularly want discussed and instruct the group to make decisions about the remainder: 'This scene involves father, mother and daughter. The mother has just found out that the daughter has been seeing a boy who has something of 'reputation' locally, although the daughter has been hiding the fact that she is seeing him. The mother has just told the father about this when the daughter comes back home after an evening out. Decide what kind of 'reputation' the boy has and why the girl has not told her parents about him.' Provided that the whole discussion is not side-tracked—which is always a possibility and not necessarily a bad thing—then it will probably concentrate on the position of the daughter *vis-à-vis* the family group and on locally received opinion about ways in which boys and girls should or should not conduct themselves. The teacher could, alternatively, delineate the situation in such a way that the preliminary discussion would be led towards a consideration of the different relationships the girl has with her father and her mother: 'When the mother tells the father about this, there is a disagreement between them about it. They are in the middle of this when the daughter comes in. Decide why the parents disagree and what each of them believes. Decide how each of them should behave towards the girl when she comes in.'

### 7.5.2 After the improvisation

The discussion that follows an improvisation can be shaped directly or indirectly by what the teacher asks the group to do.

1 He may suggest that they try to reach some general conclusion (for example, about the way in which parents behave in the matter of boy-friends). This will usually necessitate personal reminiscence as evidence.
2 He may then ask the group to invent a scene which embodies their conclusions, for presentation to the rest of the class. This has the advantage that the general and theoretical are brought back to the specific and practical.
3 He may set the groups specific topics for discussion which can then be reported back to the whole class by a representative of the group.
4 He may ask the group to make specific judgements about the behaviour of the characters in their scene (for example, opinions of the rights and wrongs of the way in which the father and the mother treated the daughter and so on).
5 He may ask them to decide what were the most important and relevant features of the behaviour of each of the protagonists and then to reshape the scene for performance to the rest of the class so that these features are emphasized. This is a useful means of concentrating the group's discussion on the essentials of the situation—and it can lead to the realization that they are dissatisfied with the whole pattern of behaviour in the scene.
6 He may ask them to go more or less straight into a follow-up scene in which the consequences of what happened in the previous one are worked out. (For example, 'Now do the scene between the boy and girl after the family row you have just done. Before you start, decide how you think the girl should present it to the boy.') In this way discussion is kept at a very practical—and often personal—level.

## Notes

1 It is possible to get into all kinds of tangles when you try to analyse that goes on when an actor portrays a character. For our purposes it is useful to think of the actor's person or self as a bundle of role-playing experience and possibilities linked to a self-image and related to an ideal self. An imagined character—if fully realized by the actor—would be built up in much the same way. Some of the components of this imaginary character will be common to the real self of the actor. To this extent there will be overlap. Sometimes—more often than not—the imagined character will not be fully detailed beforehand and the actor will be left to use his own personality where he feels this to be consistent with the demands of the character. To the extent that he does this there will be overlap. The overlap may be as slight as

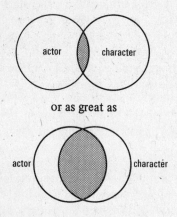

or as great as

*Figure* 7

But there will always be overlap and, in the kind of drama I am advocating, the actors will usually have a fairly clear working distinction between themselves and the characters they are playing, while the audience (if there is one) will often find that distinction very difficult to make.

2 The ideal self 'is a future goal to be striven for. It need not be unattainable; for some people it is just a little better than the actual self; when it is attained, the ideal self is then revised upwards a little. It may refer to positions and roles to be occupied, or to personality traits.' (Argyle, 1969)

3  Jourard (1968) argues that self-disclosure to 'significant others' is a vital way in which a person can realize himself and live a healthy life:

self-disclosure, letting another person know what you think, feel, or want is the most direct means (though not the only means) by which an individual can make himself known to another person.

4  What I have in mind here is the kind of 'humanities' lesson that can turn into a series of reminiscences in which the pupil enjoys the new freedom of discussion by indulging in a series of semi-fictional anecdotes, because there is insufficient shape or internal discipline to the lesson itself. This is not to say that I believe that the teacher should constantly be intervening to 'keep the discussion to the point', but I have known over-earnest Nuffielders be taken for a ride by somewhat more sophisticated teenagers. The formal constraints of preparation → improvised situation → discussion make this not just less likely but unnecessary. Apart from anything else the centre of such a lesson unit is *intended* to be fictional. (Ironically, as a result one often gets served up with fact.)

5  Dramatic improvisation is concerned with what we discover for ourselves and the group when we place ourselves in a human situation containing some element of desperation. (Heathcote, 1967)

This is not a definition that is sufficiently comprehensive for present purposes, but it is a useful one to think about if one finds the work of a class becoming complacent or predictable.

6  Argyle (1969) has a chapter on group structure which provides a useful analysis.

# 8
# Expression

## 8.1 The school play

The commonest form of expressive drama, or theatrical communication, to be found in most schools is still the school play. Even now, secondary heads can be heard to say: 'Ah, yes, we have a fine tradition of drama here. Last year we did *Oliver* and the year before it was *The Pirates* . . . , no, that was the year before, that year it was . . . .' The standard of drama in the school is indicated by the record of productions, of public performances to parents and friends. Yet this is clearly not the meaning that has been attached to 'drama' in this book, or the meaning that most specialist teachers would adhere to. Is there, then, some connection between this existing tradition and the 'new' work in drama, or are they completely and finally antipathetic? To answer this question, we must first consider what the values—and drawbacks—of school plays are.

Officially they are praised, often in much the same way as a good school football team or a successful open day. Unofficially they are a bore to nearly everyone not directly involved. The friends of the cast and the producers may be genuinely interested in what goes on. Yet very few of the people who attend school plays ever go to the theatre for pleasure. Unless the school is exceptional, you see a higher standard of acting and direction at the local rep., however mediocre, and find more of interest in an average evening's TV viewing.

Many teachers who produce school plays would readily agree—so why go on doing them? Some are forced by headmasters, the 'tradition of the school', and so on. Others, however, do so because they think it is the only way to achieve some of the following benefits:

1  Prestige for the subject
Drama teachers often feel insecure and even persecuted. Some hope that

by participating in, or even initiating, a school play they can achieve a better deal for their subject.

2  Recognition for children who are good at drama

Those who are good at games get recognition in assembly, and those who are good writers get recognition in the school magazine. So why should those who are good at drama not get similar recognition?

3  Interdisciplinary co-operation

Drama is one of the arts, and should be working hand-in-hand with music, woodwork, painting, and so on. This is difficult to organize within the curriculum (time-tabling problems, and so on), so the best chance would seem to be an extra-curricular activity such as the school play.

4  The opportunity for genuine theatrical communication

Theatrical communication is different from other forms of communication such as writing, and it is valuable experience for children. Even children who do regular, time-tabled drama benefit from the change of emphasis involved in a theatre project.

5  Stimulus and opportunities for synthesis

The production of a play provides a focus for a wide range of drama activity, especially if improvisation is used as a rehearsal method; it introduces material that might not be suitable for classroom use, perhaps because of its scale or complexity; and it provides a goal to encourage and direct effort.

6  Contact with parents and other children

Parents should know and understand what children are doing, especially in a subject like drama which is new and where there are no exercise books to be taken home and perused by mum and dad. The school play provides such contact, however inaccurately it may reflect the work actually being done in the classroom. Children from different classes are also enabled to see each other's work in drama.

While the subject politics implied in (1) may be necessary, they should not use children in this way. The second point suggests an uncertainty about the teacher's own standards and a lack of confidence in the personal satisfaction that children will get out of classroom drama. Co-ordinating the arts (3) is undoubtedly desirable, but to do it through the school play is to get it on the cheap, and in a way that often leads to as much interpersonal irritation as inter-departmental co-operation. The last three points, however, are all valid, and to abandon them completely would make the work done in class seriously incomplete. In the remainder of this chapter these three reasons for performing to an audience will be discussed in detail.

## 8.2 Theatrical communication in the classroom

How does this work on theatrical communication relate to work on improvisation discussed so far? Obviously many of the points made about work in Chapter 6 and 7 will apply here too: situations will have the same components; there will be preliminary work involving solo and group work, movement and discussion. In fact much of the material for work on theatrical communication scenes will often come from work already being done. When you are working on analytical improvisation, for example, a lesson can usefully be rounded off with a piece of theatre: 'Right, decide what you think are the rights and wrongs of factory situations like this and make up a scene to get across your opinions on the subject. Use the characters you've got or make up some new ones.' Again, work on exploration can often lead to performance: 'Think up the situation that best sums up what Richard is really like and prepare it to perform in front of the rest of the class.' Similar assignments may come out of thematic work in English or humanities: 'Prepare a scene for the rest of the class, entitled "Prejudice" ' (see the lesson extracts in 8.4.1).

However, if we ask children to prepare a scene or sequence deliberately for performance, even if only to the rest of the class, there will be different emphases in the work that is done, and particularly in the form of instruction and discussion. In the initial discussion the stress will be on the constructive and communicative aspects of the activity. Instead of asking the class to 'work out' or 'try out' a situation in which certain characters are faced with certain problems, the teacher asks the class to 'prepare a scene' which 'illustrates' or 'gets across' what their 'opinions', 'thoughts', 'feelings', or 'impressions' are about a subject, situation, character, or problem. In the discussion that follows a performance the rest of the class changes from being 'sympathetic observers', as they are in other work, to being quite specifically audience. Before, the discussion used the performed situation as a starting point for a sharing of experience by pupils who had all been working on the same or very similar situations; now, the performed scene is the end-product and the rest of the class are consumers who are in a position to judge the quality of that product. The teacher thus leads the class towards the consideration of questions such as:

What are they trying to get across?
How successful were they?
What means did they use?
How did these methods contribute to the overall effect?
Are there ways in which their message could have been conveyed more effectively?

One of the teacher's responsibilities, both during group work and in the discussion, is to help pupils to become more articulate about what they are doing and why it may be going well or badly. There seem to be three general ways of talking about these performance scenes.

1 Total message/overall impression
One can act as a kind of sounding-board and give the group as accurate an account as possible of the effect their work has on a 'representative audience', taking into account the total impression and the way in which one perceives the parts in relation to the whole.
2 Literary/dramatic
One can use the vocabulary of dramatic criticism to analyse the structure of the scene, talking in terms of character, mood, tempo, climax, and so on. (A useful modern and simple introduction to this terminology is to be found in Styan, 1971.)
3 Technical/theatrical
One can consider the way in which a piece has been staged and presented at the practical and theatrical level, and discuss physical grouping, actor/audience relationship, use of available space, and so on.

(Hodgson and Richards, 1966, contains a useful chapter on approaches, entitled, 'Dramatic Shaping and Communication'.)

## 8.3 Frameworks

Class projects in theatrical expression may consist simply of individual scenes prepared and performed for internal class consumption. If we wish to develop longer or more complex projects, however, we need some kind of framework upon which to build. Sometimes this will be chosen at or near the beginning of a section of work, while at other times it will gradually become obvious as classwork proceeds. A framework has to fulfil two needs: it must supply adequate coherence both for those working on the project and for any future audience and also it should suggest areas for further development if the original impetus of the project begins to flag.

### 8.3.1 Story and play

The most obvious framework for a project of this kind is clearly a story-telling play, just as the most obvious source of material is the existing written story or play. This is not to suggest that the aim should be to 'act out' or 'dramatize' a story that already exists. Nothing could be further from the experimental and expressive work in drama that has been discussed so far. Rather, the story or play is used to satisfy the twin needs of structure and stimulus. It provides a store of characters, situations, and spoken language from which the group can develop their own improvised scenes; and it ensures a structure to which the sequence of scenes they develop may be firmly attached. To begin with, therefore, the most useful material will be of a loosely-knit episodic structure, with a large number of clearly differentiated characters, many different scenes and opportunities for the invention of new material.

The following example shows how a story can be used as a centre and source of material from which to develop a scene for performance. A first year group, working on the well-tried biblical story of the Flood, produced the following scene, based on the characters of Noah and his three sons and their different approaches to designing an ark.

(*Ham enters, looks around. He looks thoughtfully at a plan he is carrying. He nods his head wisely. Shem comes in, also carrying a plan. He looks at Ham's plan.*)

SHEM That's wrong. It shouldn't be like that.

HAM Of course it should.

SHEM It shouldn't—look. (*Shows his own plan.*) You should paint it blue anyway.

HAM What's wrong with pink?

SHEM Pink's a fairy colour. You should paint it blue.

HAM Why blue?

SHEM Blue's a nice colour. Anyway I like blue. (*He looks at Ham's plan again.*) And that structure should be stronger.

HAM  It's strong enough.

SHEM  No, never. (*Pause.*) That's not right, never.

HAM  (*Quiet but determined.*) That's right.

SHEM  Look at my plans. Go on. They're better'n yours. Much better. Look. Structure's good, everything's good on my plans.

(*At this point Japheth enters dreamily.*)

What do you want?

JAPHETH  Dunno.

SHEM  Oh I mean fat lot of help you are. (*To Ham.*) Look—if you had a structure like that you'd be all right.

JAPHETH  (*looking vaguely at Shem's plan.*) Flat bottom no good. (*He drifts away again.*)

SHEM  Look, we don't want a flat bottom, we want a nice curved one with a good wood structure, not with you—

(*Enter Noah.*)

NOAH  'Ere what's all this argument about?

SHEM  These two won't listen to me.

JAPHETH  Eh?

NOAH  What's up? What's up—?

SHEM  (*indicating Ham*). He won't agree with my great ideas and *he* (*indicating Japheth*) doesn't know nothing.

NOAH  (*to Shem.*) What's your idea anyway?

SHEM  My idea's to have a good wood structure with blue paint.

NOAH  No, no I don't agree. I don't agree with nothing.

SHEM  Why not?

NOAH  I don't—I like my colour, green.

SHEM  Green?

HAM  Green.

NOAH  (*pointing to Japheth*). What does *he* want?

SHEM  Oh he doesn't want anything.

HAM  He doesn't know what he wants.

(*At this point a confused argument breaks out, eventually topped by Noah.*)

NOAH  Look! Pack it in. We'll have green.

HAM  Green?

JAPHETH  All right then.

(*More confused talk.*)

SHEM  (*topping it*). Look—we'd better do it your way then.

NOAH  Yes.*

107

An example of the use of a traditional play as a framework is given in the description of the 'Everyman' project in 8.4.2

### 8.3.2 The theme

Work in improvised drama can also be related to a central theme, just as work in English sometimes is (improvisation can also be used as a contributory activity to a theme in English or humanities).[1] A thematic (or eclectic) approach will probably extend beyond specific instances, and inform much of the work of a successful teacher. Thus work on the story of Noah (above) drew on a variety of source material: The New English Bible; a B.B.C. 'Drama Workshop' tape of electronic music; the poem 'The History of the Flood' by John Heath-Stubbs.

A thematic project by a group of 14- and 15-year-olds entitled 'Moneytime' incorporated the following material and types of activity.

| | *Stimulus* | *Activity* |
|---|---|---|
| 1 | 'Money' from *Dark Side of The Moon* by Pink Floyd | three separate but simultaneous dance routines: abstract, based on rhythm of music only semi-representational, on ideas about materialist society in song fantasy about fruit machines taking over the world |
| 2 | the 'bank manager' ideas outlined in Chapter 6 | three improvised scenes |
| 3 | rather repetitive piece of instrumental rock music (untitled) | dance routine based on factory machines and those who operate them |
| 4 | newspaper item about miners' strike then going on, and 'I am a man' from 'Quadrophenia' by The Who | improvisation in four scenes about bus-drivers being put out of work by miners' strike |
| 5 | | from this the cast went into interviewing the audience with microphones, all of which were dead, except for one, which sometimes broadcast what was being said |
| 6 | improvisations based on how the time of day affects the way we behave | actors set up furniture for a house, and a large clock face; members of the audience are invited to set the clock, specifying 'a.m.' or 'p.m.', and the actors have to improvise a scene illustrating that particular time of day for a family |

| | Stimulus | Activity |
|---|---|---|
| 7 | 'Lord I have time' (prayer/poem by Michel Quoist) | spoken by girl in cast |
| 8 | 'Time' from *Dark Side of the Moon* by Pink Floyd | surrealist nightmare dance drama about being trapped in time and escaping, only to find that one has crawled into another 'time cage' |
| 9 | 'Fidele's Song' and electronic music from a B.B.C. 'Drama Workshop' programme | solemn funeral dance, and recitation of 'Fear no more the heat o' the sun' (*Cymbeline*) |

*Figure* 8

## 8.4 Polishing

Story, play, and theme all provide a useful framework within which the teacher and the class can work on a project, providing stimulus material for the work to begin, and material for the teacher to feed in from time to time to keep the impetus of the project going.[2] Projects involving theatrical communication, however, also depend heavily on what is often referred to as 'polished improvisation'. Once the project is established, the problem is, just how does one polish, and how much? No direct answer can be given to such a question, since it is a matter of individual judgement which can only develop over time. All that can be done is to suggest different ways in which details can be polished and worked on, and ways in which the teacher can be involved in the process. The accompanying examples may indicate some of the underlying reasoning.

### 8.4.1 Leaving it to the group

Ideally the polishing should not involve the teacher at all, but be left to the group of children who devised the scene in the first place. With talented and/or experienced children this can be very successful. Some time ago I left a group of 14-year-olds to work on their own on the theme of 'Intolerance'. They asked to have a cassette recorder to help them with their work, and three versions of the scene were left on the tape so that others were later able to observe their work in progress. The tape gives a fascinating view of the polishing process taking place without outside interference. The two extracts come from the first and third versions.

*First version*

(*A living room. Father and Mother are sitting watching TV. Their young sons, aged 8 and 6, rush in talking excitedly.*)

CLIVE  Dad! Some new neighbours have just moved in across the street.

FATHER  New neighbours?

CLIVE
KEVIN   Yeah!

KEVIN  And he says he's gonna buy us ice-cream when he comes up.

CLIVE  Yeah.

MOTHER  We'll go and see them soon.

FATHER  Yeah. We'll make a cake.

CLIVE  Gonna ge' ge' ge' we're gonna ge' some comics and things.

FATHER  We'll go tomorrow night. You remind me, all right? To go in and see them.

KEVIN  Yeah. He's going to buy him a big tub and I'm getting a big big boat.

CLIVE  Fruit boat.

KEVIN  Yeah!

MOTHER  That's very nice.

(*Some confused talk.*) What are they like really?

KEVIN  (*tones of great enthusiasm*). Nice black man . . . .

CLIVE  Yeah—very nice.

KEVIN  With a white wife. Ever so nice he is.

FATHER  *What*?!

CLIVE  A white woman . . . 'n' . . . 'n' . . . .

MOTHER  A coloured man?

KEVIN  Yeah!

CLIVE  . . . 'n' . . . 'n' . . . I took him some flowers.

KEVIN  Yeah!

MOTHER  Where did you get the flowers from?

CLIVE  Your garden.

(*Confused talk.*)

FATHER  There are black people just across the street?

KEVIN  (*still talking about the flowers*). Some nice big ones. D'you want one?

CLIVE  His son's white.

FATHER  (*to his wife*). Why didn't you tell me about this?

MOTHER  I didn't know the house was for sale.

CLIVE  His sons—

KEVIN  What's the matter?—
FATHER  Call the real estate people.

*Third version*
(*Opening as before.*)
KEVIN  I'm going to see him tomorrow.
CLIVE  Yeah—a very nice man.
KEVIN  I'm going to bring my friend round as well.
CLIVE  Dad! There's new . . . new neighbours.
MOTHER  New neighbours?
KEVIN  Yeah.
FATHER  Really?
CLIVE  Just across the road—you have a look.
(*Father and Mother move across to the window.*)
FATHER  Where?
KEVIN  Over there.  CLIVE  Have a look.
FATHER  That's very nice. We'll have to go over to see them tomorrow huh?
MOTHER  Yes, I'll bake some cakes to—
FATHER  Good idea.
KEVIN  Make a lot because he's got a big fat boy.
CLIVE  The lady likes cakes.
FATHER  Yes. We could have a housewarming party.
(*General agreement.*)
CLIVE  She likes lots and lots of flowers because I gave her some.
MOTHER  Call in at the off-licence and get us some drink.
KEVIN  Can we come?
CLIVE  I gave her some lovely flowers.
MOTHER  What are they like ?
CLIVE  Well they . . . they . . . they're nice. They give us toys and comics and ice-creams.
KEVIN  Yeah.
CLIVE  A nice black man.
KEVIN  They're going to give me a big, big—
FATHER  *WHAT*!!!
CLIVE  A nice black man
MOTHER  *Black*?!
CLIVE
KEVIN  Yeah!

FATHER  You're kidding.
CLIVE  No.
KEVIN  No.
CLIVE  Toys and things.
(*Pause while Mother and Father go to window to peer.*)
FATHER  They are—they're black. Just across the street. Why didn't you tell me about this?
MOTHER  I didn't known.
FATHER  Well, call the real estate agent. We'll be out tomorrow.*

Considerable improvements have been made. The first version does little more than establish the general structure of the scene, providing minimal build-up to the central double-take by the father. Beyond this the detail is confused and the scene is characterized by overlapping. In the third version there is a much longer and more detailed build-up (the parents' initial enthusiasm about new neighbours, their desire to be sociable, and so on). In addition they have added the revealing and very funny details of both parents rushing to the window to peer across the street to find out if what they have been told is true.

### 8.4.2 Working in class

More often, however, especially in the early stages, the teacher has to help a group shape and polish their work. The lesson that follows was with a third year group who were working on a version of the medieval play *Everyman*. The structure, which had been shaped by the teacher, retained the medieval framework (such as Everyman's dialogue with Death, and his soliloquies) but all the intervening scenes, between Everyman and the various qualities he has to encounter, such as Kindred, Goods, and Fellowship, had been invented. The class was not in general a happy one, since most of them had opted for drama negatively because they wanted to avoid doing German, rather than for any positive reason. So progress was slow. The following extract, from work on Kindred, shows the process of developing a scene clearly and in detail. The group had been given this section of the scenario

> EVERYMAN  Lo, Fellowship forsaketh me in my most need.
> For help in this world whither shall I resort?
> It is said, 'In prosperity men friends may find

Which in adversity be full unkind.'
Now whither for succour shall I flee,
Sith that Fellowship hath forsaken me?
To my kinsmen I will truly
Praying them to help me in my necessity.

IMPROVISATION

An odious, large but credible (just!) family, exhibiting the cloying and demanding aspects of family life without any of the accompanying love and willingness to accept the faults of others. It is the occasion of some family celebration. Everyman arrives and is greeted by all. Many and gushing professions of family love all round. Then Everyman tells them that he has to go to judgement and make the pilgrimage to death. Immediately those who have professed family love melt away until he is left on his own.

After some preparation, one group produced this scene.

(*The sitting room. Father is sitting reading the paper. Mother is reading a book.*)

FATHER Dora, make us a cup of tea, please.

MOTHER Oh make it yourself. I'm reading this book; it's ever so good.

FATHER (*as son enters*). Hullo, James.

SON Shut up, I tell you, my name isn't flipping James. (*He sits and puts his feet up on the table.*)

FATHER That's what we flipping christened you—James. (*Pause.*) What you been doing?

SON I dunno. I just been up the road to the rec' . . . with these blokes.

FATHER What blokes?

SON Oh, some of these blokes.

SON (*to father*). I've had more friends than you've had hot dinners, son, so shut up.

FATHER I bet you all of those were girlfriends.

SON You were just as bad as me when you were young, so belt up.

FATHER And where did you get those shoes from?

SON Down the drain. Where do you think I got them from?

FATHER And how much did they cost you?

SON Eleven quid.

FATHER Eleven quid—all that money. I could have had a good old booze up.

SON That's your hard luck, isn't it?

GRANDFATHER (*as he enters room*). Come on, Elsie. Help us to the loo.

113

SON  Oy Mum, get us a cup of tea. Hurry up.
MOTHER  No.
SON  I said get us a cup of tea and hurry up.
MOTHER  Your sister's getting one.
SON  All right then, hurry up.
MOTHER  (*to daughter*). Look, take your gran to the loo.\*

The children involved clearly feel exposed and so are showing off by means of a kind of silly vulgarity; but they are also genuinely short of ideas and don't really know where to go or what to do. The silliness of the scene has, however, to be dealt with first:

TEACHER  Now what's the point of this scene, Michael (*the son*)?
MICHAEL  I dunno.
TEACHER  It was going in a particular direction. What were you trying to get across?
MICHAEL  I dunno, that's how we planned it.
(*Some confused talk.*)
TEACHER  Well, what have we got? We've got a group of people who don't like each other very much and they're rather offensive. Correct? Would the audience agree that they were rather unpleasant people?
(*Some general agreement form rest of class.*)
TEACHER  Right, OK, what's the point of the scene, though, as far as the script's concerned? It doesn't just say present a group of unpleasant people . . . .
ANNE  You said the other day you wanted an un-normal family.
TEACHER  All right, well, when people are not friendly in a family how does it show itself?
PETER  They don't talk to each other.
TEACHER  Don't talk to each other? Well, if we examine what Michael did, for instance, is that the way it shows itself usually, by putting your feet up on the table and—
MICHAEL  That's what I do.
TEACHER  That's what you do, if you're in a bad mood at home?
MICHAEL  Sometimes.
BRIAN  He's a liar, he doesn't.
TEACHER  He doesn't? All right, what does he do, then?
BRIAN  Just sits around on a chair.
MICHAEL  How does he know?
TEACHER  And he sulks?

114

BRIAN Yeah. He just sits there and sulks.

(*Some argument breaks out between Michael and Brian.*)

TEACHER All right, well what does the father do when *he's* in a bad mood in this family?*

The whole class were then given an exercise in pairs—son/father or daughter/mother—in which the parent wanted the child to do a household task when the child wanted to go out. One of the pairs from the original group then produced this scene:

(*The kitchen, Mother is getting tea. Daughter comes in.*)

DAUGHTER Mum, I'm going to the pictures tonight.

MOTHER I want you to clear out your room.

DAUGHTER No, I can't.

MOTHER Yes. It's in such a state. It's all upside down. The bed's not made or anything.

DAUGHTER It'll have to wait till tomorrow.

MOTHER No, it can't. Go up and do it straight after you've had your tea.

DAUGHTER Oh look there won't be time.

MOTHER Yes, there is.

DAUGHTER I'm not going to do it.

MOTHER You are before you go out.

DAUGHTER I'm not.

MOTHER You are. It's in such a state. It's all dirty and you can hoover and dust it—

DAUGHTER I'm not doing that.

MOTHER And—

(*While this scene had been going on, the original 'father' had been given instructions by the teacher. The two girls were not expecting this. At this point he comes in, from work.*)

FATHER Oh shut up. Get my tea ready.

MOTHER It's on the table.

FATHER I've had a terrible day at work.

MOTHER Oh I bet—lazing about in the loo half the day reading the paper.

FATHER Yeah. Where's the paper?

MOTHER Where you left it.

FATHER Where did I leave it?

DAUGHTER Dad, can I go to the pictures tonight?

MOTHER  No, she's got to clean out her room, hasn't she?

FATHER  Yeah.

DAUGHTER  No.

MOTHER  See. You heard what your father said.

DAUGHTER  I don't often go to the pictures.

MOTHER  You've been twice already this week.

TEACHER  (*interrupting*). Right, Grandad's just woken up and he wants his tea.

(*Grandfather goes into kitchen and sits down.*)

FATHER  Hurry up and make the tea.

MOTHER  Go and read your paper.

GRANDFATHER  Haven't . . . haven't . . . haven't . . . you got any tea for me?

MOTHER  No.

GRANDFATHER  Oh . . . make my tea . . . my back's killing me.

FATHER  As usual.

MOTHER  Oh here you are, here's a cup of tea.

GRANDFATHER  (*very weak*). Oh . . . could you lift it up to my mouth, please?

MOTHER  No, I can't. Don't be so lazy.

GRANDFATHER  It's cold.*

At this point the family is beginning to take some sort of recognizable shape and we have a basic situation that is capable of being developed. The class then followed this pattern of work:

1 One at a time the following details were added to the scene:
a A friend actually calls for the daughter to go out.
b The grandfather is made even more unpleasant and demanding.
c The knowledge that there is an uncle whom they have not seen for some time, called Everyman.

2 The scene was then re-started and Everyman, having been instructed by the teacher, knocked at the door before the daughter's friend arrived and was invited in. This scene broke down, largely because of the problem of introducing into a socially realistic scene like this the religious predicament in which Everyman finds himself.

3 Class discussion established how Everyman might present his problem to the family. This led to the following version of the scene.

DAUGHTER  Hullo, Mum, I'm going to the pictures tonight.

MOTHER  No, you're not, you're going to clear out your bedroom. You're not going out with it like that.

DAUGHTER Me friend's coming at seven o'clock.

MOTHER You haven't made your bed for about a week.

DAUGHTER Well, it's your fault that is.

MOTHER It's not. I've got everybody else's to do, including grandad's.

DAUGHTER There's nothing wrong with doing mine.

MOTHER You're old enough to do your own bedroom now.

DAUGHTER Oh mum.

MOTHER You haven't done it for about a month.

DAUGHER You said a week just now.

MOTHER That was since you've changed your bed—let alone the rest of the room. It's smothered in dust.

DAUGHTER Yeah. I'll try and do it before I go.

MOTHER No you're not. You're not going.

DAUGHTER Yes I am.

MOTHER You're not. Anyway eat your tea.

DAUGHTER I'm not hungry.

MOTHER All that wasted food.

FATHER (*entering from work*). Where's my tea? I've had a horrible day at work.

MOTHER Sitting on the loo reading the paper.

FATHER Where's the paper?

MOTHER Where you left it.

FATHER Where's that?

MOTHER How should I know? You're the only one who reads it.

FATHER (*going to cupboard*). Oh yeah. It's still here. (*He accidentally knocks a chair over.*)

MOTHER Pick these chairs up.

DAUGHTER Dad, can I go to the pictures tonight?

FATHER No you can't, you've go to clear up your room, haven't you. (*Enter Grandfather.*) Hullo Grandad.

GRANDFATHER (*trying to sit down*). Hullo ... oooh ... oooh ... oooh ... me back's got worse .... (*He finally sits down.*) ... Can I have a cup of tea, please? ... and a saucer. (*He is passed a cup of tea. He starts drinking it noisily.*)

FATHER Revolting old man.

(*They all watch him fascinated.*)

FATHER Eeeerh!

DAUGHTER Oh come on. I've got to go now.

MOTHER No, you're not going.

DAUGHTER Me friend's coming in five minutes.

MOTHER Well you're not going.

(*There is a knocking at the door.*)

DAUGHTER That's probably her now.

(*She goes to the door and opens it. It is Everyman.*) Oh hullo.

EVERYMAN Hullo.

DAUGHTER Come on in.

(*General round of 'hullo's'*)

FATHER Oh, it's me old brother-in-law.

GRANDFATHER It's . . . good . . . good . . . to see you.

MOTHER Where you been then?

EVERYMAN I've been in Australia.

MOTHER Australia?

EVERYMAN Yeah—going around a bit.

MOTHER You look miserable.

GRANDFATHER Yes you do, from what I can see.

MOTHER Yeah, what's the matter?

EVERYMAN Nothing.

MOTHER Lost your job?

EVERYMAN No.

MOTHER There must be something the matter.

EVERYMAN Well . . . there was this bloke come and told me I'd got to die.

MOTHER Die? That's stupid.

EVERYMAN I've got to go on this pilgrimage and give a . . . reckoning . . . of my life and sins and what good I've done and . . . you know . . . I want someone to come with me to keep me company . . . . When you go there you never come back.

GRANDFATHER My back wouldn't make it.

DAUGHTER Well, I've got to go to the pictures. (*Exit.*)

FATHER Well . . . well . . . coming down the pub, Grandad?

GRANDFATHER Pardon?

FATHER Coming down the pub, Grandad?

GRANDFATHER Yes, half past three.

FATHER No, are you coming to the pub, Grandad?

GRANDFATHER Oh yes . . . pardon?

MOTHER Off you go.

(*They exit.*)

(*To Everyman.*) I can't really come with you . . . . I've got to look after all of them . . . especially Grandad.*

The ending still needs some tidying up, but the scene has now been developed into something approaching its final shape, and the main intention, of providing a somewhat critical account of a certain kind of family life within which Everyman's rejection by 'Kindred' will make sense, has been largely fulfilled. The process involved a number of elements:

questioning by the teacher
class discussion
analytical work in pairs
building up from pair work by adding characters
practice.

### 8.4.3 Producing a script

In the first example of 'polishing' the teacher had to do nothing except set things in motion, while in the second he had to work hard, suggesting alternatives, questioning, devising working methods to extend the pupils' work. Often, however, the teacher finds himself in some intermediate position, where the group needs some help with a scene, but not too much. A modified version of the approach illustrated in 8.4.2 can be used, or the scene can be developed into a script. In order to do this, the teacher needs to tape-record the lesson (see 9.6). The improvised scene is then transcribed, and 'polished' on paper. This really only works when the tidying up is on a relatively small scale.

The scene that follows also comes from the 'Everyman' project, which included a number of brief scenes illustrating some of the Seven Deadly Sins. Four girls, given 'Gluttony' to work on produced this scene:

(*A smart restaurant. Two large women, A and B, are sitting at a table, attended by the waitress.*)
A  (*looking at large menu*). Ooooh minestrone.
B  Oxtail and chicken.
A  That'll be for the first course.
B  Rump steak.
A  Chicken.
B  Ye-es.
A  I'll have two if they're extra large.

B   And some chops.
A   Yes, yes, providing they're—
B   Yes, 'n onion.
A   Yeah, 'n cauliflower, cabbage, onions.
B   Peas.
A   Peas, yes. Parsnips.
B   Yes.
A   Mashed potatoes, chips.
B   Roast potatoes.
A   Oh and Bisto gravy.
B   What for pudding?
A   Oh-um-chopped bananas and some strawberries.
B   That'll be enough.
A   Oh and two cups of coffee.
B   Oh and two doughnuts.
A   And two chocolate eclairs.
WAITRESS   That's for the two of you?
BOTH   No . . . each!*

This scene needed to be short, making its definition of Gluttony neatly and economically. What the girls produced was nearly there, with a good touch of surreal humour. Only a little trimming was needed to produce this script:

A   Soup.
B   Yes, tomato.
A   Minestrone.
B   Oxtail . . . and chicken.
A   Main course.
B   Rump steak.
A   Chicken.
B   Yes, and roast beef.
A   And chops.
B   Yes, chops.
A   Large ones.
B   Veg.
A   Yes, veg.
B   Cauliflower.
A   Cabbage.
B   Brussels and peas.

A  Onions and carrots.
B  Parsnips.
A  Yes, parsnip.
B  Roast potato.
A  Mashed.
B  Chips.
A  Chips.
B  Now for pudding.
A  Ice cream sundae.
B  Strawberries and cream.
A  Yes, and two cups of coffee.
B  With cream.
A  Biscuits and cheese.
B  Fruit.
A  After Eights.
B  Yes, After Eights.
WAITRESS  (*sarcastically*). Is that all?
A  Yes, we only wanted a snack.
WAITRESS  For the two of you?
BOTH  Each!

Part of the interest is now in the economy of the dialogue, so that the three girls could learn the actual words written. If more detail were involved, the script might merely serve as a reminder for the actors of the details that were essential, while they still improvised the conversation itself. (The question of how script is used once it has been developed is treated again in 9.4.)

## 8.5 Performance

Such projects as those outlined above may or may not be initiated with eventual performance to outsiders in mind, but it is important that all those concerned know that the decision about whether to set up a performance will not be taken until a fairly late stage, when both material and actors are ready. In my experience, there is nothing more destructive of useful work than the knowledge that, willy-nilly, a performance of some kind has got to be given on a certain date. Thus the classroom projects that we have been describing cannot normally be expected to lead to performances on the scale of the school play, since the school play normally has to be arranged too far ahead. What this work can lead to, though, is presentations of a relatively informal kind to parents and/or other pupils in the school. The following discussions, therefore, are based on the assumption that any performing done by children will derive from their experience of theatrical communication within their own class or drama group and that they will not be exposed to any wider audience until the teacher has determined not only that they are ready for it, but that their work will actually benefit from it. Performances will then be affected by considerations of audience, space, staging, and style of presentation.

### 8.5.1 Audience

If theatre is concerned with communication, considerations of the nature and size of the audience will inform not only production style, but also the material chosen, the way it is organized, the staging—everything. If we do not have at the front of our minds the particular people with whom we wish to communicate, then we will fail as communicators. This thought is obvious enough, yet it is not always at the front of the minds of those who produce plays. The size and composition of the audience, therefore, must be determined by the needs of the performers. The first audience that pupils experience should not be much larger than the class in which they have been accustomed to working, so that one concentrates on the difficulties of presenting work to people— usually parents or another class of the same year—who have not been closely associated with its development, but who still have sympathy with and understanding of the performers. When this initial difficulty has been coped with, one can start thinking of audiences that are larger and more diverse.

### 8.5.2 Space

Most schools have a multi-purpose hall, but few have special accommodation for dramatic performances. The school hall, however, has connotations of publicness and spectacle (not to mention religion and morning assembly) that one usually wants to avoid, and halls are generally too big for the small-scale intimate performance which will frequently be given, especially at the beginning. If a performance for an audience of, say, 40 is put on in a hall that will seat 400, the total effect can be chill and dreary in the extreme. Far better to find a room with floor space of, say, 1000 square feet and give a third of it to the audience and two thirds to the actors. Existing light or a few spot-lights on stands, either plugged in direct to the wall sockets or to a small portable distribution board, can be used. It is best to keep things as simple as possible, since the electrical and electronic hardware associated with drama has an unpleasant habit of taking over from the human subject-matter.

### 8.5.3 Staging

From audience, space available, and subject-matter come considerations of staging—the physical relationship between actors and audience. The audience can be on one, two, three, or four sides of the actors:

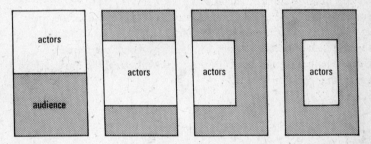

*Figure* 9

Different shapes for the acting area can be experimented with:

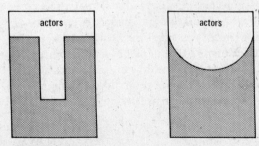

*Figure* 10

123

And there can be more than one acting area:

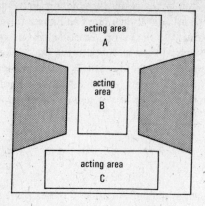

*Figure* 11

The choice that is made will affect not only how much space is available
for acting, and the size of the audience, but also the effect that the
performance will have upon the audience, and the effect that the audience will have upon the actors. The inter-relationship is too complex
to be dealt with here (see Joseph, 1967, on theatre in the round), but
careful thought and experiment in classwork will reveal the implications
of a particular form of staging.

### 8.5.4 Style of presentation

Obviously the overall style of a project is not just a question of staging
but involves decisions about the total meaning of what is presented.
The same basic situation may be presented, with different emphases, as
farce, comedy, satire, or tragedy. If the project is narrative, the viewpoint that is chosen and the kind of scene that is shown as well as the
montage of scenes will all contribute to the impact of the performance
upon the audience. A study of how theatre works to communicate (see
Styan, 1963 and 1971) will help, but experiment in the classroom will
also be of benefit. Television can also be studied easily.

## 8.6 Conclusion

There has been a traditional view amongst drama teachers that 'drama' and 'theatre' are so divided from each other as to be almost antipathetical. This distinction is more theoretical than real. The practising secondary teacher will find it more useful to consider that classroom improvisation draws upon three functions of imitative behaviour—exploration, illustration, and expression—each of which can productively contribute to the others. It is important, however, to remain aware of the precaution that lay behind the drama/theatre distinction: children do not benefit from too much exposure too early, and may even suffer because of it. Particularly when working on expressive improvisation, the teacher must consider very carefully the degree to which children should be exposed to an audience at any particular stage of experience, and work to avoid the pitfalls involved.

### Notes

1  A wealth of thematic ideas for dramatic work with younger children is contained in *Children and Themes* by Alan Lynskey (1974) in the present series.

2  I am not a great believer in John Allen's idea that 'In its content drama is self-creative and self-perpetuating' (Allen, 1974), which he originally propounded in the Department of Education and Science Survey, *Drama* (H.M.S.O., 1967). Such a philosophy strikes me as dangerously optimistic—even sentimental—in its view of human nature. Teachers would be unwise to base their lesson planning on the assumption that the materials for their lessons will be 'self-creative' and 'self-perpetuating'. The philosophy may work with self-selected groups, such as a school drama club (or the students of Mr. Allen's Central School of Speech and Drama), but it would foolish to rely upon it with an ordinary (and therefore random) secondary class.

# 9
# Software

## 9.1 Instructions spoken and written

In the early stages of drama work, the class will usually be totally dependent upon spoken instructions and suggestions from the teacher. The initial novelty of the activity is normally quite enough for the class to cope with, without the further complication of handling pictures or scripts and interpreting their contents. So the class bases its work initially on the familiar (perhaps too familar) voice of the teacher, and any materials used will be for the teacher to read and interpret to the class.

Quite soon, however, written material has to be used in class. There are three main reasons for this. The first concerns the degree of complexity children can take when they are given instructions orally. Drama is unusually dependent upon spoken instructions: the participants have to listen intently in order to pick up not only what they are to do, and how they are to organize it, but also the material they are to use, often without any visual back-up at all. In schools of a more traditional mould, such intent listening is not often required because of a greater emphasis on written language. (Most other subjects use textbooks to amplify the teacher's oral instructions, which can thus be reduced to the economical 'Open your books at page 20'.) So the teacher may find it difficult to get complex instructions across to the class. Whenever instructions reach a degree of complexity beyond what the class can tackle aurally, it is necessary to support what the teacher says with written material. Secondly, the use of written instructions makes it possible to have a wide range of class organizations with different groups working on different sets of material and at different speeds. Thirdly, oral instructions put severe limits on the diversity and richness of material that can be employed. As soon as one wants to provide material that is to be contemplated and discussed before group improvisation takes place, then it is essential that the pupils have the written material in front of them.

Why, then, are so many drama teachers often loth to use written material at all and why are there not more successful drama 'course books' on the market? The reasons for this are illustrated by the following extracts from a drama course book designed for use by first year secondary pupils. The introduction for pupils explains:

The passages between △ and △ are action sequences. Once you have read the material between the triangles, leave the book behind and start exploring the ideas which come from it.

Section 1, 'The Mind's Eye' then begins:

In this sequence, your teacher will ask you to carry out certain directions:
△ Look about you.
  Remember three objects.
  Close your eyes.
  Can you remember No 1?
                No 2?
                No 3?
  Now open your eyes.    △

Clearly this is material that pupils do not need in written form, even if they could read it with their eyes closed! Such books at this stage of drama work are just a hindrance. The teacher can give the instructions orally just as well—indeed, he has to—and the books are merely a distraction. As the book continues, the problem becomes more acute:

When you are working and it is necessary for everyone to stop at once, your teacher will say 'HOLD IT', which means 'stop what you are doing and keep your position still', and then 'RECOVER' which means 'return to your normal listening position'.
△ Imagine you are a barker and trying to attract a crowd. Find an action area. Get up high.
  STAND BY                ACTION
  HOLD IT                 RECOVER   △

Meantime, what happens to the books? Are they put down after the passage between the triangles has been read? In which case they litter the floor or there is a hiatus while they are put neatly away and another when they are 'recovered'. Or do the children take them to the 'action' area? In which case the books either clutter that piece of floor space, or the children hold them while they are trying to act, thus inhibiting the movement of one hand. A more serious problem is that the less confident child will be under temptation to refer to the book in the course of the action, rather in the way one might use a cookery book.

These are not intended as criticisms of just this particular course (Yates and Hornby, 1974), which also contains some interesting material. Rather, they illustrate one of the problems that any drama course is up against: in the early stages, and whenever the proportion of instruction to action is relatively low, written material is a nuisance. It is only useful when children have got used to the activity and to organizing themselves within it, and when more complex and diverse material is needed.

## 9.2 Written directions

So far the emphasis has been deliberately on instructions. This is not to imply that teachers exist to direct everything that children do, but to make it quite clear that whatever form written material may take, its function in improvisation is as a communication between author and reader (teacher and pupil, playwright and actor) about what kind of activity to engage in, or what starting point to take. This applies also to full script: the script itself is not the play, but rather 'instructions about how to make a play', a distinction that many English teachers still find difficult.

The first kinds of written material to be used, however, are less likely to be script than different kinds of directions for groups to follow. These can be divided into two groups: shared instructions (the scenario) and special instructions (individual/group worksheets).

### 9.2.1 The scenario

Instructions that are shared by the whole group often take the form of a scenario—that is, a set of notes about a situation, the problems and relationships it contains, and the course it follows. Some or all of the following information may be given:

1 List of *characters* with notes on sociolinguistic role and personality of each.
2 Notes on *relationships* relevant to the work being done.
3 Any other relevant background information, especially the *underlying problem.*

4  For each situation the
*location*
*time*
*starting point*
notes on the *progress* of the situation, often divided into working sections.

If the whole of this information were to be given in some detail, the
scenario would be lengthy and probably inhibiting, leaving little to the
imagination and initiative of the group. Detail is particularly limiting if
the scenario deals with a sequence of interdependent situations, because
then situation A has to end in such a way that situation B can develop
from it. This is appropriate if a theatre project based on a known story
is being developed, or if the scenario is used as a means of recording
work that has already been developed in a freer way by the group (see
9.6). For the exploratory function of improvisation, however, it is far
too restrictive. Much of the time, therefore, some of the information
listed above will be provided, but not all. The 'gaps' will determine both
the subject-matter for the group's preliminary discussion and where
they have to exercise their imagination (see 7.5.1).

### 9.2.2 Individual and group assigments

Sometimes one wants to simulate real life by having actors go into a
situation with different attitudes and expectations (see 6.3). This can
be achieved by dividing written instructions between a general worksheet of which everyone has a copy, and separate worksheets which are
special to individual actors. An example will show how this works in
practice.

*General worksheet*
Mr. Brownsell (Jim) in his 40s, until recently employed at Maybury and
Campbell printing works. Now unemployed.

Mrs. Brownsell (Pat), housewife, helps out part-time in local primary
school canteen.

David, their son, is 16 and an engineering apprentice.

Mary, their daughter, is in the fourth year at school and wants to stay on
into the sixth form.

129

In context

Issue: Mary has been staying out at local youth club until after 11 p.m. and both her parents think it is too late.

Time: 11.25 p.m.

Place: the Brownsells' living room.

Starting point: Mr. and Mrs. Brownsell are sitting watching TV. David is reading a magazine. Mary is still out. They hear her opening the front door.

*Individual worksheets*
*Mr. Brownsell*　You think it's a father's job to be strict. If Mary can't be persuaded to see sense, then it is your job to *make* her. It's no good leaving it to your wife any more—she has tried often enough and failed.

*Mrs. Brownsell*　You think Mary is being silly, but you know from experience that it's no good forcing her. If you can talk to her on her own you might be able to make her see sense, but you know that your husband is too heavy-handed and only makes things worse.

*David*　It's about time Mary started to see sense. Father's right in a way—although he does go on. All you want to do is go back to your electronics magazine.

*Mary*　Everybody else stays at the youth club until eleven at least. Both your parents are being silly about it. Father is too bossy by half and Mother is all right, but she worries far too much.

This assignment produced the following improvisation:

MARY　I've had the most beautiful time.
MOTHER　Where've you been?
MARY　Down to the youth club.
FATHER　Good was it?
MARY　Yes it was beautiful.
FATHER　Five hours. You've been out five hours. You said three hours and you'd be back. Ten o'clock you said.
MARY　All right—the time went by so fast.
FATHER　You could at least have let us know you were going to be late, couldn't you?

MARY  We don't have a telephone, so how could I call you?

FATHER  You said you'd be back at ten and you're back at twelve. What's your excuse? Come on.

(*Pause.*)

MARY  I dunno. I just had a good time and I didn't realize what the time was.

DAVID  Just leave her alone, Dad. I was out that late before and you never got onto me. Why are you getting onto her?

FATHER  It's time something was done.

MARY  What do you mean?

FATHER  You've been out hundreds of times before and you've been late as today, and all the other times you've had made-up excuses. Where's your one this time? Where's your excuse?

DAVID  Excuses? Can't you think of—

FATHER  You be quiet when I'm talking!

(*Long pause.*) Was the taxi late, did you miss the bus?

MARY  Well I . . . .

FATHER  Did you?

DAVID  Oh shut up, Father, just let me read my book.

FATHER  Get out . . . get out.

DAVID  No.

MOTHER  (*very quietly to daughter*). Come on dear, I want to speak to you . . . .

MARY  But why? I haven't done nothing wrong.

MOTHER  Yes you have—you've been out five hours. You're supposed to have been out three, now come on.

MARY  Everyone else can stay out.

(*General commotion. Father topping it with*)

FATHER  But you're not everybody else, are you? Anyway what do you reckon you are?

DAVID  (*to Father*). Well, what makes you different to everyone else?

MOTHER  Look, keep your mouth shut and don't speak to your father like that.

DAVID  Oh you shut up.

MOTHER  You shut up.

FATHER  (*to son*). You reckon you're it, don't you? You've got a job, haven't you? You're an apprentice, aren't you?

DAVID  Yeah, well?

FATHER  You reckon you're it.

DAVID  Well, so what?

FATHER  I've . . . I've had forty years—

(*Confused argument.*)

MARY  I'm not going about any more if this is going to happen.

FATHER  You're not, oh no, you're not.

DAVID  She can go if she wants to.

FATHER  Get out. Get out. Get out and stay out. (*Bundles son out of the room.*)

(*To daughter.*) And you. You're not going out again until I decide you're responsible to go out. Three hours is all I—

MOTHER  Don't talk to her like that. Shut up.

FATHER  It's about time something was done. You let her get away with it far too many times.

(*Confused argument.*)

MARY  All you ever do is argue.

MOTHER  How old is that child? You tell me, how old is she?

FATHER  She's still at school.

MOTHER  It doesn't matter.

FATHER  You've let her get away with too much.

MOTHER  She has not got away with it—*

At which point the Headmaster came into the studio and the improvisation ended.

## 9.3 Diversity and enrichment

As well as enabling instructions in improvisation to be more complex, written material can provide stimuli that will set pupils' imaginations working and details that will contribute to the depth and solidity of the improvisation. Especially when one moves from analytical role-playing to the fuller exploration of inter-personal contexts, it is impossible for the teacher to provide sufficient stimulus material simply in spoken instructions. Sometimes, too, the group's own imaginative response and relevant experience are too limited to provide them with sufficient material to work on. Different kinds of written material can then be used to open up and enrich both initial discussion and subsequent improvisation. Suppose a group is working on the problems of old age and the difficulties of communication; then the two short pieces that follow would provide very different starting points for improvisation:

When the literary gentleman, whose flat old Ma Parker cleaned every Tuesday, open the door to her that morning, he asked after her grandson. Ma Parker stood on the doormat inside the dark little hall, and she stretched out her hand to help the gentleman shut the door before she replied 'We buried 'im yesterday, sir,' she said quietly.

'Oh, dear me! I'm sorry to hear that,' said the literary gentleman in a shocked tone. He was in the middle of his breakfast. He wore a very shabby dressing gown and carried a crumpled newspaper in one hand. But he felt awkward. He could hardly go back to the warm sitting room without saying something—something more. Then because these people set such store by funerals he said kindly, 'I hope the funeral went off all right.'

'Beg parding, sir?' said old Ma Parker huskily.

Poor old bird! She did look dashed. 'I hope the funeral was a—a success,' said he. Ma Parker gave no answer. She bent her head and hobbled off to the kitchen . . . .

(From 'The Life of Ma Parker' by Katherine Mansfield.)

> I have something to tell you
> I'm listening.
> I'm dying.
> I'm sorry to hear.
> I'm growing old.
> It's terrible.
> It is, I thought you should know.
> Of course, and I'm sorry. Keep in touch.
> I will and you too.
> And let know what's new.
> Certainly, though it can't be much.
> And stay well.
> And you too.
> And go slow.
> And you too.

('Two Friends' by David Ignatow)

## 9.4 Script

Written work in general creates certain problems in drama but makes possible large extensions of the work that would otherwise be impossible. Script even further increases the difficulties and widens the possibilities. The difficulties are greater because script means the imposition of exact words to be spoken. There are really only three things you can do: you can ignore this fact and treat the script just like any other piece of writing, and use the contents without the form; you can read it holding the piece of paper or book in one hand; or you can learn it. Whatever refinements may be suggested, these are the only logical possibilities and they all involve limitations of freedom.[1] Ways of approaching these problems, and the advantages that will ensue from using script, are best seen in relation to the different forms that script can take when it is being used as an aid to improvisation.

### 9.4.1 Snippets

One way to use a very short script extract has already been described in 6.2.1. The advantage of an extract of only three or four lines is that it can be fairly easily memorized in a few moments in class. (Indeed, it can be written up on a chalkboard or a large sheet of paper and displayed so that all can see it.) Groups can then be asked to improvise away from or towards it. In other words, the short extract may be used as a stimulus and a starting point:

Work out a scene that begins like this:
A Must you go now?
B Yes I must.
A Please stay . . . .
B No.
A Why?

Or it may be used to shape the whole scene:

Work out a scene that ends with the following words:
A You never let me do what I want.
B Don't talk to me like that—
A I hate you!

### 9.4.2 Unallocated script

Such snippets impose a considerable amount of detail on the actors; in particular they determine how many characters there are and who says which words. It is, however, possible to devise a set of words that are not allocated to characters and that can in fact be allocated and even arranged in a number of different ways. The group is presented with a 'block' of sentences which they then have to arrange for as many characters as they think suitable, according to what they think the situation is 'about'. This technique has been used by Derek Bowskill in a number of publications and the example that follows comes from *Workshop One–Circus Fairground Zoo* (see Chapter 10). The text begins:

It was all your fault things went wrong tonight
I was doing my best
But you would insist on fooling about
You were showing off and playing to the gallery
I wouldn't call them a gallery
But you wouldn't call them a handful either

In *Young Drama* (Bowskill, 1973a) he writes:

There is no story line to be unearthed, and any final meaning(s) of the piece will depend upon the locale and characterization created by the students . . . .
 Simply by selecting and rejecting lines (for themselves as individuals or for the whole group, since there is no reason why parts of the text should not be jettisoned) the students are exploring the basis of dramatic character and/or personal identity . . . .
 The following divisions suggest one or two ways of using the texts:

ONE  It was all your fault things went wrong tonight
TWO  I was doing my best
ONE  But you would insist on fooling about
TWO  You were showing off and playing to the gallery
ONE  I wouldn't exactly call them a gallery
TWO  But you wouldn't call them a handful either

ONE  It was all your fault things went wrong tonight
       I was doing my best
       But you would insist on fooling about
       You were showing off and playing to the gallery
TWO  I wouldn't exactly call them a gallery
ONE  But you wouldn't call them a handful either

ONE  It was all your fault things went wrong tonight
TWO  I was doing my best
THREE  But you would insist on fooling about
FOUR  You were showing off and playing to the gallery
TWO  I wouldn't exactly call them a gallery
ONE  But you wouldn't call them a handful either

The benefits of such a method are obvious, and it is not difficult to devise other material along the same lines.

### 9.4.3 The 'mixed' scenario

The advantage of a short script extract can be combined with those of the scenario so that key sections of dialogue are incorporated into the outline notes for a situation. This is particularly useful if the actual words spoken are of real significance in the definition of the situation—whether for their literal meaning or for the light they shed on character, mood, and so on. The technique is used to considerable effect by David Adland in *The Group Approach to Drama* (see Chapter 10). The following extract comes from a scenario based on 'The Doctor and the Devils' by Dylan Thomas, in *The Group Approach to Drama 4.*

*Plan of Action*
1  Mr. Webb knocks at the door of the lodging house. He carries a bundle in a stick over his shoulder and holds a little boy by the hand. Mrs. Webb carries a baby in a shawl.
MRS. WEBB  It's a poor, dirty place.
MR. WEBB  It's got a roof.
MRS. WEBB  I think I'd rather be on the roads, sleeping in the hedge in the cold . . . .
2  Kate opens the door. She is wearing a new shawl. She demands two-pence for a bed. Mr. Webb gives her a coin from his bundle and they follow her in.

The combination of snippet and outline make certain qualities of a scene more specific and detailed, without scripting the whole thing. However, it has the disadvantage of the full scenario, in that rather a lot of the scene is determined beforehand. Such material, therefore, is more useful for developing a theatre project from a known story than for exploratory improvisation. It is is also useful for the teacher who wants a class to work towards an understanding of how to use a full script.

### 9.4.4 Scripted scenes and whole plays

It is not within the scope of this book to consider how improvisation may be used as a means for producing whole plays or long extracts from plays. The fullest available account of this process remains Hodgson and Richards' *Improvisation* (1966). Since this is based on experience with highly selected groups of students, and even with these it was not nec-essarily successful, it is to be applied with care to the average secondary school. The book also slides over certain important aspects of the trans-ition from improvised version to full script.

For present purposes, the script is merely another way in which improvised situations may be psychologically and linguistically enriched. Therefore, in practical work, the script has to be broken down, whether by the teacher or by the group, into sections that can be assimilated. Large snippets can be extracted and worked on in the ways already suggested, or the whole scene can be turned into a mixed scenario. Obviously, the more the teacher can leave these processes to the working group, the more its members are going to learn, not only about the play, but about the relationship between their own view of life expressed in their improvisations and that of a playwright expressed in a scripted scene. Fascinating (and very detailed) examples of the ways in which a complex script may be approached in improvisation are to be found in David Adland's book *The Group Approach to Shakespeare* (see Chapter 10).

## 9.5 The use of recorded sound

A scene may also be enriched and detail provided to stimulate imagination by the use of recorded sound.

### 9.5.1 Recorded speech

Types of material that are useful include:

1 Dialogue extracts from a recording of a play.
2 Extracts from radio actuality material (news bulletins, interviews, commentaries).
3 Presentation of other stimulus material by more than one voice (choral speech, chants, fictional arguments).
Such materials have an immediacy and vividness that cannot be matched by the printed page, and they can be used with pupils who cannot read very well. They do, however, normally limit the class to working together on the same material at the same time, and, as with the more conventional spoken instructions by the teacher, there is a limit to the amount that can be assimilated at one hearing.

### 9.5.2 Effects

Sound effects can also be used very powerfully, both to stimulate
imagination at the start of a piece of work ('Listen to these sounds and
then work out the scene that they suggest to you') and also as a significant feature occurring in a scene ('Listen to these sounds and then work
out a scene in which they occur'). Such work follows naturally from
exercises based on listening (see 3.2.2).

These effects may be live or recorded. Teachers may make their own
recordings, or use those commercially available. The B.B.C. publish an
excellent series. Since the copyright restrictions are generally relaxed
on such records, many of them can quite legitimately be taped so as to
lengthen a particular effect, or to superimpose two effects. It is also
permissible to use them in public performance.

### 9.5.3 Music

The recent use of electronic sound sources, especially by progressive
pop groups, has led to a kind of transitional area between sound effects
and music. The Pink Floyd, for example, use real sound, electronic
sound, and acoustic music to produce pieces that are more like sound
collages than conventional 'songs'. Such material is a very useful way in
to the use of music as a stimulus for improvisation and movement work.
Some of the other less commercial pop groups, in common with many
folk singers, pay considerable attention to words, and the context of
the songs can also be useful in improvisation. Thus, without going into
the realm of 'pure' movement and dance drama, there are two main
ways in which music can be used in improvisation:

1 As a starting point to establish general or specific subject-matter.
Both sound synthesis and the more conventional song can do this.
2 to suggest or reinforce mood—either before work begins or as a kind
of background to a scene as it is being worked through.

## 9.6 Making a record of the improvisation

In discussing improvisation we must also consider how the drama lesson
itself may generate written and recorded material.[2] A great strength of

improvisation is its impermanence. Every improvisation is unique, with all the accompanying possibilities of freshness, vigour, enthusiasm, and imagination. The improvisation is, too, private to the group in which it takes place. Impermanence, however, has its drawbacks. In particular, if we want to analyse what has happened in a particular improvisation, teacher and actors have no common ground to which to refer. The teacher (and anyone else watching) knows what the whole improvisation looked like from outside. The individual participant only sees it from inside. He may or may not remember accurately what the others did and said, but his observation is heavily conditioned by the demands of his own role. Thus when we discuss an improvisation with our pupils we are not all talking about the same thing, in the way that an English teacher and a pupil are when they discuss a piece of writing. In addition, after a lesson has finished, the teacher has nothing but his memory to guide him when considering what happened and planning what to do next. For these and other reasons it is occasionally useful, for both the teacher and the group, to have some kind of record of improvisations that have taken place.

### 9.6.1 Uses for the teacher

A fundamental part of any teacher's job is the evaluation of what is done by an individual, a group, or a class and the subsequent planning and preparation of fresh materials and activities. In improvised drama, evaluation is usually based upon the teacher's observation of the improvisation as it takes place. Some improvisations, however, would benefit from a more leisurely consideration. This is possible if either a video- or an audio-recording is made. The obtrusive presence of bulky recording equipment will obviously affect what takes place in an improvisation so that a video-recording can become somewhat artificial. (See Appendix.) The most convenient technique is certainly the audio-recording made unobtrusively, though not necessarily surreptitiously. (If you try to make recordings secretly you will probably get found out sooner or later and, in any case, by definition you cannot discuss the results afterwards with the class. My experience is that an 'open' recording of work is soon accepted and then ignored, provided that it *is* unobtrusive and that its purpose is understood by the pupils.) The resulting recordings can be used as they are, or they can be transcribed as many of mine have been for this book. Either way, they have several uses:

1 They enable the teacher to evaluate work in more detail.
2 They enable teacher and class to discuss an improvisation on a more equal footing.
3 They concentrate attention on the verbal elements of a scene.

When transcripts are made, other uses may be made of the material:

1 The relation of spoken language to written can be discussed.[3]
2 One can use the whole 'script' or parts of it with other classes, or with the same class later.
3 Such transcripts also help to bring home the frequent disparity there is between children's spoken and written linguistic achievement. In schools where spoken language is undervalued this can be useful.

### 9.6.2 Use by groups

When a group of pupils is developing anything more than the simplest and most straightforward situation, and certainly when they are concentrating on theatrical questions, they often have continuity problems. If a piece of work spreads over several lessons, with gaps of a few days between them, each new lesson frequently entails considerable backtracking to pick up the threads of what was done the previous week. The process can be considerably shortened, if not eliminated, by making some kind of record of each scene, in the form either of a scenario, or of an audio-recording. If the group wishes, the tape can then be transcribed and worked up by a writer into a full-blown script as was done in the 'Everyman' project (see 8.4.2). The initial value of the record, however, is to jog the memory.

A group can also use a tape-recording to evaluate its own work in much the same way that a teacher does. After each version of a situation, they can listen to the tape and discuss it before organizing and effecting refinements. It was in this way that the scene on 'Prejudice' in 8.4.1 was developed.

### Notes

1 Hodgson and Richards (1966), who advocate a very extreme impro-

visatory rehearsal system for even the most complex full-length plays, conveniently slide over the transition from improvising the substance of a scene to actually using *all* and *only* the words the playwright has given the characters. Indeed, their whole argument seems a little disingenuous at this point.

2 This subject is treated more fully in 'Recording the Drama Lesson' (Seely, 1974).

3 Along the lines described in the *Language in Use* units C1, C2, C6, C7, C9 (Doughty *et al.*, 1971).

# 10
# Resources

With the rapid expansion of educational publishing, it is increasingly difficult to keep in touch with all the relevant material in any subject area. Currently available, there are over twenty books directly relevant to drama teaching at the secondary level, and many times that number which touch upon some aspect of it. The problem lies in knowing which book or set of materials is likely to fulfil the needs of an individual teacher. The purpose of this chapter, therefore, is to point out what is available and to attempt a classification of the types of material that different writers and publishers present. The first two sections, dealing with books for teachers on theory and practice and with teaching materials, are intended to be as comprehensive as possible, and any omissions are accidental. The remaining sections, concerning script and other resources, are selective, and the idiosyncrasies of choice are my own. I am grateful to all those publishers who have given me information about their lists and review copies of relevant books.

## 10.1 Books for teachers

The first part of this section gives an analytical table of books concerning the theory and practice of educational drama in the secondary school. In the second part the books are listed with details of publication and a short description of contents and approach.

### 10.1.1 Analytical table

The following categories need to be detailed:

| | |
|---|---|
| Age groups | Rationale |
| Activities described | Lists of resource material. |

*Age groups*
Obviously age groups cannot be precisely specified, and where there is
any doubt an age group has been excluded rather than included.


*Rationale*
The four categories are roughly as follows:

1  Psychological
Those approaches which concentrate on what is going on inside the
participant, rather than on the social nature of the activity.
2  Sociological
Approaches which are primarily concerned with social relationships in
a sociological way, or at least systematically. This category overlaps
considerably with 'psychological' and 'linguistic'.
3  Linguistic
The general attitudes towards language described in the present book.
4  Theatrical
The rationale has in large part been derived from the needs and experiences of the theatre.


*Activities described*
'Exploratory improvisation' is used to cover both analytical and exploratory work (as described in this book). 'Theatre arts' refers to the 'craft'
side of the theatre: the mechanics of staging any performance for an
audience, from the viewpoint of both actors and backstage workers.


*Lists of resource material*
The numbers in this column relate to the following:

1  List of useful addresses and organizations, plus detailed information
about National Drama Organizations.
2  Appendix describing work of Bristol Street Theatre Troupe ('A do-it-
yourself kit').
3  'Checklist: Performing a Play', plus list of useful names and addresses.
4  Glossary of terms.
5  List of major suppliers; list of suitable plays; note on school drama
festivals; glossary of terms.

| Figure 12 Books for teachers | Age group | | | Rationale | | | | Activities | | | |
|---|---|---|---|---|---|---|---|---|---|---|---|
| ● forms an important part of text  ○ forms a part of text  — not a relevant consideration | 11–13 | 13–15 | 15+ | Psychological | Sociological | Linguistic | Theatrical | Relaxation/games | Concentration/sensitivity | Movement | Voice |
| Acting and Stagecraft Made Simple | | ✓ | ✓ | ○ | | | ● | ● | ● | ● | ● |
| Approaches to Drama | ✓ | ✓ | ✓ | ● | ○ | ○ | ● | | | ○ | ○ |
| Child Drama | ✓ | ✓ | | ● | ○ | ● | ○ | ○ | ● | ● | ○ |
| Creative Drama in Schools | ✓ | ✓ | ✓ | ● | | | ○ | ○ | ○ | ● | ○ |
| Development Through Drama | ✓ | ✓ | | ● | | | ○ | ○ | ● | ● | ● |
| Drama and Education | ✓ | ✓ | | ● | | | ● | | | ● | ● |
| Drama Casebook | ✓ | ✓ | ✓ | ● | ○ | ○ | ○ | ○ | ○ | ● | ● |
| Drama in Education | — SEE NOTES — | | | | | | | | | | |
| Drama and Theatre in Education | — SEE NOTES — | | | | | | | | | | |
| Drama and the Teacher | ✓ | ✓ | ✓ | ● | | | | ○ | ● | ● | ● |
| English Through Drama | ✓ | ✓ | | | | ○ | ● | | | | |
| Exercise Improvisation and Inprovisation Steps Out | | ✓ | ✓ | | | | ● | | | | |
| Improvisation | | ✓ | ✓ | ○ | ○ | | ● | | ● | | ○ |
| Improvisation for the Theater | ✓ | ✓ | ✓ | ○ | | | ● | ● | ● | | |
| Improvised Drama | ✓ | ✓ | ✓ | | | ● | ● | | | | |
| Introduction to Child Drama | ✓ | ✓ | | ○ | | | | | | ● | ○ |
| Movement, Voice, and Speech | | ✓ | ✓ | ○ | ○ | ● | ○ | ● | ● | ● | ● |
| Play, Drama, and Thought | ✓ | ✓ | ✓ | ● | ● | ● | ● | — | | |
| The Play is not the Thing | ✓ | | | ○ | | | ○ | ○ | ○ | ○ | ○ |
| The School Play | | ✓ | ✓ | — | | | | | | | |
| A Space on the Floor | ✓ | | | ● | | | ● | | ● | ● | |
| Teaching Drama (Clegg and Pemberton-Billing) | ✓ | ✓ | ✓ | ● | | | | | | ● | ● |
| Teaching Drama (Courtney) | ✓ | ✓ | ✓ | ● | ○ | ○ | ○ | | | ● | ● |
| The Uses of Drama | ✓ | ✓ | ✓ | ● | | | ● | — | | |

| described | | | | | Organization | | | | Examples of pupils' work | | Lists of resource material | | | | |
|---|---|---|---|---|---|---|---|---|---|---|---|---|---|---|---|
| Exploratory improvisation | Expressive improvisation | Projects | Scriptwork | Theatre arts | Lesson planning | Studio and classroom organization | Relation of drama to social context of school | Relation of drama to rest of curriculum | Verbal quotation | Photographs | Actual teaching materials (including sample lessons) | Teacher's bibliography | Lists of teaching resource material | List of records | Other resources |
| ● | | | ● | ● | | | | | | | ○ | ○ | | | ○ 1 |
| ○ | ○ | ○ | ○ | ○ | | | ○ | ● | | | | ● | | | ● 2 |
| ● | ● | ● | ○ | ○ | | ○ | ● | ● | ● | ● | | | | | |
| ○ | | | ○ | ● | ○ | ○ | ○ | ○ | ○ | ● | | ○ | | ● | |
| ● | ● | ○ | | | ○ | ● | | ● | | | ● | ○ | | ● | |
| | ● | | ● | | ○ | ○ | | ○ | | | | | | | |
| ● | ● | ● | ● | ● | ○ | ○ | ● | ○ | ● | | ○ | | | ● | |
| | | | | | | | | | | | | | | | |
| | | | | | | | | | | | | | | | |
| | | | | | | | | | | | | | | | |
| ● | | | ● | ○ | ● | ● | | | | | ● | ● | ○ | ● | ● 3 |
| | | | ● | ● | | ○ | | ● | ● | | | | | | |
| ● | ● | | ● | | | | | | | | ● | | | | |
| ● | ● | ○ | ● | | | | | ○ | | | ● | ○ | | | |
| ● | ● | | | | ● | ● | | | ○ | | ● | ○ | | | |
| ● | ● | | ● | | | | | ○ | | | ● | | | | |
| ○ | ● | ○ | | | | | | | ● | ● | | | | | |
| ● | | | | | | | | | | | ● | ○ | | | ● 4 |
| | | | | | | | | ○ | | | | ● | | | |
| ○ | ○ | | ○ | ○ | ○ | ○ | ○ | ○ | | | ● | ● | | | |
| | | | ● | ● | | | ● | | | ● | | ● | | | ● 5 |
| ● | ● | ● | | ● | ● | ● | | ● | ● | | ○ | ● | ● | ● | ● 6 |
| ● | ● | ● | ○ | | ● | ● | ○ | ○ | ● | ● | ● | | | ● | ● 7 |
| | ● | | ○ | ● | ● | ○ | | ● | | | ● | ● | | | |
| | | | | | | | | | | | | | | | |

6  Notes on mask-making; the use of CCTV; speech and drama sylla-
buses; list of useful addresses.
7  Notes on equipment and furnishing; list of useful scripted plays.


## 10.1.2 Detailed list of books

**Acting and stagecraft made simple** by Derek Bowskill
W. H. Allen 1973
Specifically designed for adult amateur theatre work, this contains
much that is relevant to school work, although obviously it has to be read
selectively and suitable material for adolescents chosen.

**Approaches to drama** by David Male
Allen and Unwin 1973
An 'ideas' book. Every chapter deals with the practice of drama in
school from a different angle: 'Dramatic Forms', 'Drama in the Curriculum', 'Drama and English', 'Drama and the Scripted Play', 'Drama and
the Theatre', 'Drama and the Arts'. Its value lies in stressing the diversity
of educational drama and in stimulating the teacher to think and work
beyond the limits of his current personal range.

**Child drama** by Peter Slade
University of London Press 1954
Fundamental to the study of the development of educational drama.
Slade begins with a careful observation and analysis of children playing,
and continues to show in detail how the school may provide facilities
and encouragement for child drama. The discussion is clearer and more
detailed about the primary age range than about the secondary. Under-
standably, after twenty years, the book seems a little dated.

**Creative drama in schools** by Gabriel Barnfield
Macmillan 1968
Written by a practising teaching, it contains particularly useful and
sensible sections on motion, movement, dance, dance-drama, and a
lengthy section on producing plays in schools.

**Development through drama** by Brian Way
Longmans 1967
Brian Way worked with Peter Slade. He was responsible for developing
some of Slade's ideas into forms that would be both practicable and

acceptable in the secondary school. Like Slade (and Derek Bowskill) his theoretical writing tends to be couched in a very personal—even esoteric—terminology, but (also like Bowskill) he is full of practical ideas. This book probably contains more directly useable lesson material than any other listed. Its organization, however, makes it difficult to find what one is looking for without reading a whole chapter.

**Drama and education** by A. F. Alington
Blackwell 1961
A short account of drama practice in primary and secondary school, developed from the 'dramatic-literature-plus-speech-work' approach, and concentrating on expressive work. A good summary for its time, but both theory and practice have progressed since then.

**Drama casebook** by John Challen
Methuen 1973
The writer says many useful things about improvisation, play production, dance-drama, and film-making by describing his own personal experience, mainly as Head of Drama at the Thomas Bennet School, Crawley. He is, therefore, particularly interesting on the school context, the relationship of drama to the rest of the secondary curriculum (and the relationship between the drama teacher and other teachers), the experience of being a drama teacher, and the kinds of interactions with pupils involved. But the book does not set out to be a systematic guide, and is not useful in a search for lesson material or ideas on how to plan a course.

**Drama in education** edited by John Hodgson and Martin Banham
Pitman
A series of regular surveys (the first two have so far appeared) containing a wide variety of writing relevant to educational drama at all levels. Relatively little that is directly relevant to classroom work has appeared, but the dialectic and theory is interesting.

**Drama and theatre in education** edited by Nigel Dodd and Winifred Hickson
Heinemann 1971
The report of the 1969 Clifton College Drama Conference. A good cross-section of drama theory and practice at the end of the sixties, this is mainly of historical interest. It does contain one interesting, if difficult, paper by Dorothy Heathcote.

**Drama and the teacher** by Derek Bowskill
Pitman 1974
Derek Bowskill is one of what might be termed the 'intense' school of
drama writers; his theoretical writing can become clotted and obscure.
His practical writing, however, is detailed and relevant, containing a
wide range of useable ideas.

**English through drama** by Christopher Parry
Cambridge University Press 1972
A personal account of work in a highly selective school, relating old-
fashioned 'dramatics' to old-fashioned English teaching. It has little to
say about classroom drama as understood here, and nothing about the
close linguistic relationship between 'English', the pupils' own language,
and improvised drama.

**Exercise improvisation** and **Improvisation steps out** by Robert G. Newton
J. Garnet Miller 1960 and 1967
Aimed primarily at the adult amateur actor and at ultimate theatre work.
On relationship, and on how to approach a script through improvisation,
they contain sensible and practical ideas and a number of useful exercises.

**Improvisation** by John Hodgson and Ernest Richards
Methuen 1966
Despite an attempt to provide a rationale for the educational applications
of improvisation, this is essentially a theatre book, concerned with the
use of improvisation to illuminate the scripted play and to develop
group theatre. Exploratory improvisation is only considered when it
relates to the play or group theatre theme. However, within these limits,
there is material that can be used in the secondary school for the purposes of dramatic shaping and communication, building characterization,
exploration of mood and feeling, and building a play from improvisation.
The final section concentrates on the use of improvisation in the production of plays.

**Improvisation for the theater** by Viola Spolin
Northwestern University Press 1963
A sourcebook of games and exercises, most of which were originally
used with older adolescent and adult groups, but which can in many
cases be applied to classroom drama. The active role of the teacher is very
clearly defined. Miss Spolin uses the concept of the 'Point of Concentration' (POC). Each exercise has one POC and the progression is based

largely upon the provision of more complex situations and more demanding POCs. She deals first with the elements of improvisation, then, after
a section on work with children, she proceeds to 'formal theater'. A very
detailed book which, although not comprehensive enough to provide a
whole course, is extremely valuable in any drama teaching.

**Improvised drama** by Peter Chilver
Batsford 1967
Largely a book of teaching material, it begins with a short, sensible
introduction about the nature of improvisation and its application in
the secondary school, seeking to debunk some of the more pretentious
claims made for it. Various different types of teaching material are
covered: improvisations based on situations (general situations, historical
events, law cases, incidents in plays, operas, and ballets); improvisations
based on excerpts from stories, novels, and plays; improvisations based
on detailed instructions to each character; and improvisation as a way
of studying a literary text or producing and rehearsing a play. These materials are sensibly selected and the comments made are useful at the
practical, classroom level.

**Introduction to child drama** by Peter Slade
University of London Press 1958
A potted version of Slade's *Child Drama*, easier to use, but not as useful.

**Movement, voice, and speech** by E. Musgrave Horner
Methuen 1970
This book seeks to break down the old barriers between voice, movement, and improvisation and to establish spoken language as central to
the whole business of acting—and living. The approach is mainly emotional and physiological. The author has a lot of sensible points to make
about spoken language and provides an intelligent and practical approach
to the development of speech in the classroom. A wide range of exercises
is included on relaxation, kinesthetic improvisation, and creative interpretation.

**Play drama and thought** by Richard Courtney
Cassell 1968
Seeking to provide a sound theoretical background to drama in educa-
tion, Courtney works through a number of broad themes (for example,
'Dramatic play and child psychotherapy' and 'Social origins of drama').
The book is heavy going, but it is the only serious attempt to provide a

comprehensive and coherent account of 'The intellectual background to dramatic education'.

**The play is** not **the thing** by Gordon Fairclough
Blackwell 1972
One of 'Blackwell's Practical Guides for Teachers', the book contains some interesting ideas, although many of them are already to be found elsewhere. It is confusingly presented, and tries to do too much in too short a space. Also the appropriateness of a particular activity to an age group is sometimes difficult to work out.

**The School Play** by Richard Courtney
Cassell 1966
Not directly concerned with classroom work, but adopting an approach that should grow out ot it, this book is described as a companion to Courtney's *Teaching drama*. It deals in depth with all the technical aspects of theatrical expression, and with the process of play selection and rehearsal, as well as characterization and working on a script.

**A space on the floor** by Colin King
Ward Lock 1972
An eclectic approach to practical drama in the middle school. The first section emphasizes exploratory aspects of improvisation, and the second expression. A lot of useful, detailed advice on planning lessons, and some informative appendices (for example, on mask-making). One chapter 'Drama Diary', is a useful account of personal experiences as a drama teacher at a secondary school.

**Teaching drama** by R. N. Pemberton-Billing and J. D. Clegg
University of London Press 1965
One of the few books directed solely at the secondary teacher. Various features which are either unique or presented with particular clarity include a detailed progress through different types of activity, a combination of general approaches with specific lesson plans, and detailed notes on how to plan a lesson and how to organize a studio or classroom. While it does not perhaps contain as many practical ideas as *Development through drama,* it is clearer and far easier to use.

**Teaching drama** by Richard Courtney
Cassell 1965
A product of what might be termed the 'alternative tradition' of educational drama (which regards theatrical expression as something to be adapted

150

and used rather than regarded with suspicion). This book contains a wide range of ideas about improvisation, voice, movement, and script work for use in both primary and secondary schools. Its drawback is that it is too wide-ranging for the available space.

**The uses of drama** edited by John Hodgson
Eyre Methuen 1972
A collection of extracts and original pieces on the themes of: the state of affairs; some basic attitudes; elements of drama; links with the subconscious; search for drama in education; and search for a new drama in the theatre. The materials are interesting, useful, and sometimes stimulating, but the stated intention of the book, to provide 'sources giving a background to acting as a social and educational force' is pretentious, if one compares it with *Play, drama and thought.*

## 10.2 Teaching materials

This section, dealing with teaching materials specially designed for improvised drama, also has an analytical table followed by a detailed list.

### 10.2.1 Analytical table

Remarks about age groups and types of activity in 10.1.1 apply also to this table. The symbols used are also the same as in Figure 12. The following categories need to be detailed:
*Format*
C cards  B book
V book with visual layout combining words, pictures and graphics in such a way that the overall impact of the page is important.
*Stimulus material (other)*
US unallocated script    M montage of elements from original script

### 10.2.2 Detailed list of books

In one or two cases books or materials are not described, because copies were not available at the time of going to press.

**Acting for you** by Joan Davenport
Blond 1971

**A chance for everybody** by John Hudson and Peter Slade
Cassell 1967

**Dramawork One** and **Dramawork Two** by William Martin and Gordon Vallins
Evans 1972 and 1973

| Figure 13 Teaching materials | Format | Age group | | | Stimulus material | | | | | |
|---|---|---|---|---|---|---|---|---|---|---|
| ● forms an important part of text<br>○ forms a part of the text | | 11-13 | 13-15 | 15+ | Prose | Verse | Script | Scenario | Visuals | Other |
| *Acting for You* | | | | | | | | | | |
| *A Chance for Everybody* | | | | | | | | | | |
| *Dramawork* | V | | | ✓ | ● | ○ | ● | ● | ● | |
| *Exploration Drama* | V | ✓ | ✓ | | ● | ● | ● | ● | ● | |
| *Expression Through Drama* | | | | | | | | | | |
| *Fact and Fiction* | V | | | ✓ | ● | ● | ● | | ● | |
| *The Group Approach to Drama* | B | ✓ | ✓ | ✓ | ● | | ● | ● | ○ | |
| *The Group Approach to Shakespeare* | B | | | ✓ | ● | | ● | ● | | M |
| *Ideas in Action* | B | ✓ | (✓) | | ● | ○ | ● | ● | ○ | |
| *Living Expression* | B | ✓ | ✓ | ✓ | ● | ● | ● | ● | ● | |
| *Playscripts* | C | ✓ | ✓ | | ● | ● | ● | ● | ○ | U.S. |
| *Stories into Plays* | C | ✓ | | | ● | | | | | |
| *Think, Move, Speak* | | | | | | | | | | |
| *Workshop One* | KIT | ✓ | | | | ● | | | ● | U.S. |

In context

These two books follow up the approach developed by their authors in *Exploration drama*, combining themes and types of activity. The first book is thus divided into the following major sections:
Workshop (methods and approaches)
Project: Elizabethan England
Penny Plain: Twopence Coloured (theatrical style)

| Instructions | | | Support material | | Types of activity | | | | | | | | | Follow-up | |
|---|---|---|---|---|---|---|---|---|---|---|---|---|---|---|---|
| Pupil | For teacher in pupil's book | Separate teacher's book | Audio | Visual | Relaxation/games | Concentration/sensitivity | Movement | Voice | Exploratory improvisation | Expressive improvisation | Projects | Scriptwork | Theatre arts | English/language | Other subjects |
| | | | | | | | | | | | | | | | |
| | | | | | | | | | | | | | | | |
| ● | | | | | ○ | ○ | ○ | ● | ● | ● | ● | ○ | ○ | ● | ● |
| ● | | ● | | | ● | ○ | ○ | ○ | ● | ● | ● | ○ | | ● | ● |
| | | | | | | | | | | | | | | | |
| ● | ○ | | | | | | ● | ● | ● | ● | | ● | | | |
| ● | | ● | | | | | | ○ | ○ | ● | ● | ● | ● | | |
| ● | | | | | ○ | | | | ● | ● | | ● | ● | | |
| ● | ○ | | | | ○ | ● | ● | ● | ● | ● | ● | ○ | ○ | ○ | ○ |
| ● | | ● | ● | | ● | ● | ● | ● | ● | ● | ● | ● | | ● | |
| ● | | ○ | | | ○ | | ○ | ● | ● | ○ | ● | ● | | ○ | ● |
| ● | | | | | | | ● | | ● | | | | | | |
| | | | | | | | | | | | | | | | |
| | | ● | ● | ● | ○ | ● | ● | ● | ● | | ○ | | | ● | ● |

153

Project: Ned Kelly
People, Events, and Ideas (documentary improvisation and theatre)
Project: Moby Dick
There is considerable emphasis on theatrical communication, and the
books would form very useful source material for, say, fourth and fifth
year CSE drama classes. They are, however, relatively expensive, and for
the most of the work at least one book between two would be necessary.

**Exploration drama** by William Martin and Gordon Vallins
Evans 1968
*Carnival* (ages 7–9); *Legend* (ages 9–10); *Horizon* (ages 10–11);
*Routes* (ages 11–13). A collage of pictures, graphics, verse, prose, and
script, plus original material by the authors. The early books derive much of
their material from myth, ritual, and children's games. The later books
increasingly use theatre forms and materials. (Thus the last book contains theatre projects based on *Journal of a Plague Year* and *War of the
Worlds,* and extracts from *West Side Story* and *Macbeth*.) A thematic
organization, with strong emphasis upon an inter-disciplinary approach.
As the detailed teacher's book is separate, the pupils' book contains
only stimulus material, and can be used as the teacher wishes.

**Expression through drama** by John Hodgson and David Blewitt
Macmillan
Not yet available. Six pupils' books and a teacher's book, to cover the
secondary age range.

**Fact and fiction** by Jerome Hanratty
Cambridge University Press 1971
Designed for older pupils. A compilation of extracts from theatre, verse,
and actuality, with suggestions for approaches to dramatic interpretation
and investigations. Useful source material for improvisation work on an
occasional basis, but lacking sufficient thematic or theatrical coherence
to make it more generally useful.

**The group approach to drama** by David Adland
Longman 1964–72
Six books plus teacher's book. The only full, year-by-year drama course
in print at the time of writing, this has deliberately limited aims. It
focuses on the pupil-organized group which plans, rehearses, and then

performs a polished improvisation. In the early stages, the stimulus material consists of a combination of story-line, character descriptions, and instructions for the pupils. As the course progresses, scenarios are developed using an increasing amount of script, and the later books concentrate on extended extracts from the scenario versions of known plays, as well as complete scripts of one or two short plays. In the later books, too, there is an emphasis upon fringe and experimental theatre. Theatre arts work is introduced in Book 4 and assumes increasing importance in Books 5 and 6.

**The group approach to Shakespeare** by David Adland
Longman 1972–
Published so far: *Romeo and Juliet; The Merchant of Venice; Twelfth Night; A Midsummer Night's Dream.* David Adland provides a range of materials and activities (although not a copy of the script itself). These are designed to deepen pupils' thinking about the text through imaginative involvement. The situations of the play are paralleled in improvised situations; the text is cut about then reassembled in stimulating montages; there are suggestions for the rehearsal of individual scenes; and quotations from reviews of the plays in performance.

**Ideas in action** by Patricia Yates and Robert Hornby
English Universities Press 1974–
A five-year/five-book course of which the first two have been published. The books cover a wide range of activities and materials: the first book concentrates on small-scale exercises and short improvised scenes, mainly for pairs and fours; the second uses improvisation to build up towards a project. The books are addressed, often clumsily, directly to the pupil, and there is frequent uncertainty of tone and audience level. For example the second book contains the script of a mummer's play, a suggestion that the pupils might like to work on Pinter's 'The Black and White' and to use a piece of dialogue in which one character calls another a 'pander' ('a male bawd or procurer', *Shorter Oxford Dictionary*). None of these suggestions really seem to hit the correct level for 12-year-olds.

**Living expression** by John Hodgson and Ernest Richards
Ginn 1968–71
The only existing English course that has improvised drama as a central activity and in which drama is developed coherently and consistently over a five-year period. The five books each consist of: 'Programme' (writing and talking, improvisation, movement and acting); 'Anthology'

In context

(poetry, prose, and script); 'Newsfile' (a scrapbook of newspaper cuttings photographs, pictures, and jottings). The material shows an admirable range and the activities are both detailed, varied, and progressive. There are also supporting records.

**Playscripts**
Kenyon-Deane
1  Senior Playscripts
*Gilgamesh—Hero of Babylon* by Derek Bowskill; *Horizons—The Saga of Captain Cook* by John Boylan
2  Junior Playscripts
*Seaventures* by Derek Bowskill; *Legends of the Seasons* by Pauline Edwardes; *Powers of the Earth* by Pauline Edwardes
Each playscript takes a central story, character, or theme and develops it through a series of cards. (Six sets of cards are probably needed for a class of about thirty.) The cards contain script, chants, prose description, unallocated script, and pupil instructions. There are some notes on organizing the work, but these are deliberately kept to a minimum. The format and the general presentation make these materials suitable for the teacher who likes a lot of freedom and is prepared to adopt an imaginative and individual approach.

**Stories into Plays** by Janet Fielding
Harrap 1973
A set of fifteen cards. Each contains a short story and, on the other side, suggestions for 'miming' and 'talking'. These are very simple and really designed for the primary age range. They would be suitable for first year remedial classes in the secondary school.

**Think, Move, Speak** by Peter Watcyn-Jones and Janina Watcyn-Jones
University of London Press
Three sets of cards: 'Mime and Movement'; 'Stories for Acting'; 'Improvisation'. Also a teacher's book.

**Workshop One: Circus, Fairground, Zoo** by Derek Bowskill
Dent 1973
A multi-media kit consisting of: tape (96 minutes); colour filmstrip; pupils' book; teacher's book. (Additional pupils' books have to be bought separately.) The centre of the kit is the tape, to which other resources relate. The tape consists of three types of material: direct address to the pupils; voice over music; 'clean' music (acoustic and electronic). It thus follows the pattern of the author's B.B.C. 'Drama

Workshop' series (vastly superior to more recent offerings) and is of value to the inexperienced teacher who wants help, especially in the development of movement work. The filmstrip is a combination of realistic and abstract pictures. The pupil's book contains a number of 'poems' by Derek Bowskill: some of these are conventionally narrative or descriptive, while others are complex, unpunctuated, unallocated verse scripts which would prove difficult for less able children but most stimulating for the more able.

## 10.3 Script

Obviously it is only possible to give a small selection of the material available. The scripts and scenarios listed here are all either edited or specially written for school use.

### 10.3.1 Collections of one-act and short plays

**Conflict In Drama** edited by John Hodgson
Methuen 1972
1 *The personal conflict*
'David and Broccoli' by John Mortimer; 'Transcending' by David Cregan; 'A Night Out' by Harold Pinter
2 *The social conflict*
'There's no room for you here for a start' by Henry Livings; 'The Kitchen' by Harold Pinter; 'Soldier, Soldier' by John Arden

**Eight Plays** edited by Malcolm Stuart Fellows
Cassell 1965
*The Boy Who Wouldn't Play Jesus* by Bernard Kops
*Ars Longa, Vita Brevis* by Arden and D'Arcy
*The Spongees* by Jean Morris
*Dare to be a Daniel* by Alun Owen
*The Island* by Frederick Raphael
*This Year's Genie* by James Yaffe
*The Man in the Case* by Rosemary Anne Sisson
*The Loot* by Gwyn Thomas
The plays are published both separately and together in one volume. Suitable for the 11–14 age group. *Ars Longa, Vita Brevis* is interesting as an improvisation scenario, written by professional playwrights.

**Longman Imprint Books**
So far in this series Longmans have published four collections of plays,
all edited by Michael Marland:
*Scene Scripts* (seven short plays)
*Z Cars: Four Television Scripts*
*Conflicting Generations: Five Television Plays*
*Steptoe and Son: Four Television Plays*

**Playbill** and **Second Playbill** edited by Alan Durband
Hutchinson
Two series, each consisting of three books of five plays, by modern
playwrights, specially for young people. All the plays were previously
unpublished and the writers include Alan Plater, Anne Jellicoe, and
David Cregan. Both series increase in difficulty between Books One and
Three.

**Student Drama Series** edited by Michael Marland
Blackie
Collections of one-act plays:
*You and Me* (four plays by Plater)
*Theatre Choice* (plays by Owen, Saunders, Whiting, Plater, and Hall)
*Laughter and Fear* (nine plays by Campton)
*Spotlight* (modern classics by O'Neill, Lady Gregory, Brecht,
Pirendello, Conrad, and Mirabeau)

**Two Ages of Man** edited by A. W. England
Oliver and Boyd 1971
Four plays about childhood and adolescence:
'The Private Ear',
'Unman Wittering and Zigo',
'The Raft of the Medusa'
'Stephen D.'
Essentially for older pupils. At least two of the plays ('The Private Ear'
and 'The Raft of the Medusa') need very sensitive handling indeed.

**Windmill Books of One-Act Plays**
Heinemann
Seven (so far) collections of one act plays, some of which are in the
tradition of little plays to read round the class, but others (especially the
sixth book) are much more in tune with modern approaches to drama.

## 10.3.2 Full-length plays

**Dramascripts** advisory editor: Guy Williams
Macmillan
A series of plays either adapted from novels, or specially written for
school use. The main inspiration tends to be literary but there is some
contemporary and social reference too (for example, *Hijack*). Nothing
revolutionary about the series, but it moves away from the conventional
school play towards something slightly freer and more adventurous.

**Hereford Plays** general editor: E. R. Wood
Heinemann
A wide range of plays edited with notes (usually literary rather than
theatrical) for school use. Mostly established modern classics (for
example, Bolt, Miller, Whiting) plus a few earlier writers (for example,
Wilde, Flecker). For the 15+ age group.

**Johnny Salter, The Car, The Chicken Run** by Aidan Chambers
Heinemann 1966, 1967, 1968
Three full-length plays written by a practising secondary teacher for his
own pupils. These plays may seem a little dated now (*Johnny Salter* was
written in 1964) but they show what can be developed from classroom
work, and they still provide useful starting points for improvised and
scripted work.

**Kingswood Plays**
Heinemann
A series of plays specially written or adapted for the 10–14 age group.
Includes simplified classics, such as *The Servant of Two Masters* and
*The Towneley Plays*.

**Methuen Young Drama**
A new series of plays either written specially for use in school or by
young people, or for theatre-in-education projects. Titles so far include:
*Playspace* (four short plays for the middle school age range) edited by
Michael Kustow
*Timesneeze* by David Campton
*Recreations* by John Challen
*How We Held the Square* by David Cregan
*Adam Unbound* by Barry Sullivan
*Thank You Very Much* by C. P. Taylor

*The Adventures of Gervase Becket* by Peter Terson
*John Ford's Cuban Missile Crisis* by the Bradford Art College Theatre Group

**Student Drama Series** general editor: Michael Marland
Blackie
Useful plays and adaptions for senior pupils:
*The Caucasian Chalk Circle* by Bertolt Brecht
*Billy Liar* by Keith Waterhouse and Willis Hall
*A Kind of Loving* by Stan Barstow and Alfred Bradley
*The Diary of Anne Frank* by F. Goodrich and A. Hackett
*The Hungry Wolves* by Romain Rolland
*The Queen and the Rebels* by Ugo Betti
*The July Plot* by Roger Manvell
*Chips with Everything* by Arnold Wesker
*The Old Ones* by Arnold Wesker

## 10.4 Other relevant teaching materials

In addition to material that has been specially prepared for drama, there is also a considerable amount of published material designed for more general work in English or humanities that uses improvisation and role-playing amongst other activities, or that lends itself to improvisation. The list that follows indicates the range of such material but is highly selective.

**Funny and moving** and **Fast and curious** edited by P. R. Smart and P. R. Goddard
David and Charles
Two entertaining and attractively produced 'scrapbooks' of ideas, quotations, comments, and activities based on a series of words. For each word a wide range of meanings is explored and there are suggestions for simple movement and improvisation. As the books currently cost over £2 each, each pupil is unlikely to have a copy. They may provide teachers with useful ideas, however.

**In other people's shoes** by Peter McPhail
Longman 1972
Three sets of cards:

1 *Sensitivity*
24 cards containing simple situations to which the individual is invited to offer the response he thinks most suitable for him personally.
2 *Consequences*
58 cards outlining situations and asking the pupil the question, 'What could happen if someone . . . ?'
3 *Points of view*
36 cards, each containing a situation involving conflict in one of five areas: sex, age, class, race/colour/culture/religion/politics, psychology. These are specifically designed for role-playing.

A teacher's book outlines the philosophy behind the materials, suggests ways in which they can be used, and classifies some of the possible responses pupils may make. The materials are open enough for use with pupils between the ages of 11 and 16, and cover that intermediate area between English, drama, religious education, and humanities that is increasingly seen to be important.

**Interplay One** by John Watts
Longman 1972
A kit of two records, three filmstrips, and a pupil's book designed to be used independently or together to provide a year's work in English and drama. It consits of 18 units, many of which are conventional English teaching themes and which are composed of prose extracts, poetry, and suggestions for discussion, writing, and drama. The drama suggestions are thoughtful and make use of both audio- and visual stimuli.

**Meet Your Future** (Books 1, 2, 3) by A. Chalmers, H. Davidson, and G. Smith
Holmes McDougall 1970–72
Material for pupils of 14–16. The emphasis is on the individual in his relationship to friends, family, and the local, national, and world communities of which he is a member. These themes are developed through passages for study and suggestions for a range of activities. There are regular suggestions for role-playing situations, both simple and more complex, but all eminently practical. A most valuable general course for ROSLA pupils (and others,too) with improvisation used as it could be more frequently in such materials.

**Pic Papers** by Eunice Boothman
Kingswood Publications 1974

A pack containing four copies each of five different broadsheets. Each broadsheet tells a story in sixteen photographs with simple captions. They are designed for remedial reading work and some of them will lend themselves readily to improvised drama with such classes. More able children, however, will probably find them too explicit.

**Scene** by Frederick Palmer
Kingwood Publications 1973
A pack of large but inexpensive picture cards with questions. There are twenty cards and each depicts a different scene. Many of them lend themselves directly to improvised drama work.

**Situations** The North West Regional Curriculum Development Project for R.S.L.A.
Blackie 1972–3
A two year course in kit form. It attempts to attack language through situations rather than in some more abstract way. The kits contain a significant element of improvisation and role-playing.
playing.

**Storypacks** by E. W. Hildick
Evans 1971
Published so far: *Cokerheaton* and *Rushbrook.*
Kits of actuality material based upon fictitious communities. The kits are presented in the form of huge books, which the teacher has to dismantle, cut up and reassemble. The 'Rushbrook' kit concerns 'a small agricultural village' and contains the following materials: a set of detailed dossiers on children at Rushbrook school; extracts from the children's diaries; a home-made 'book' about their school; letters from and to residents in the village; newscuttings (introducing specific events affecting the life of the village); an extract from the local guide book; script of a radio story by the husband of a local teacher; TV script based on the life of one of the local boys; maps of the village; views of the village 'then and now'; nearly a hundred assignment cards. There is also a short teacher's book. The idea of inventing an entire fictional community with complete documentation is a valuable one for situational work and suggests all sorts of possibilities. The 'Rushbrook' material is perhaps more suitable for upper primary work—secondary pupils might find it a little tame—but there is plenty to build on.

**Visual discussions** by David Adland
Longman 1972–74
Three books: *I am a man*, *Which Way*, and *Identity*. A challenging collage of all types of material—prose and poetry, fiction and documentary, picture and playscript—with suggestions for a wide range of activities including a number of drama projects.

# Appendix:
# the use of closed circuit television[1]

Closed circuit television is increasingly available in schools, and yet there is little evidence in the literature on drama that much detailed thought has been given to its use in ordinary classroom work. Indeed, many consider it a gimmicky and time-wasting innovation that has little long-term potential. Closed circuit television certainly brings a number of problems: the average school will only have one camera and one video-recorder, which are bulky and difficult to move round the building; the simplest improvisation seems to take hours to set up satisfactorily, and there is no guarantee that the camera will not suddenly develop a fault, or the video-recorder refuse to produce a picture; there is cable all over the place for the actors to trip over; and even when a programme is produced, it may suffer too much from comparison with broadcast television to give any sense of achievement.

Obviously, then, closed circuit television is unlikely to be of value with a class of thirty in a single, or even a double, period. However, if the teacher is able to plan for work in a block of time, with a relatively small group, he will find it a valuable teaching aid. Where closed circuit television is most useful is in rapidly recording and replaying a piece of drama, in making 'throwaway' recordings that can be used to make a point or stimulate a discussion, and that can perhaps be kept a short while for purposes of comparison before being erased. Its principal limitation is that only a small area can be covered by one camera, and that the size of the screen is also small. If the camera is removed far enough from the actors to allow the whole body to be shown, then it is covering large areas of unfilled space as well, and the human face appears minute. So the camera works most effectively in close-up. Then, however, it exaggerates the distance between things. Thus, if we are to concentrate on the upper part of two actors' bodies and if both are to appear in the same shot, they need to be almost on top of each other. So, if one wishes to work on the most expressive feature, the face, it is necessary to work with a small number of actors in a limited space with relatively little movement, as excessive and confusing camera movement should be avoided. In summary, the typical small-scale CCTV equipment that is likely to be available in a school is suitable for relatively intensive work over a planned and limited period of time, during which it is used as a teacher aid rather than as a creative medium, and the work done will involve small-cast, small-scale, relatively static situations.

In my own work, I began by regarding CCTV equipment as not much more than an ordinary audio tape-recorder with pictures added. It seemed obvious that if I video-recorded a short improvisation and then played it back before the usual discussion, there were considerable advantages, the most important of which was that those who had taken part in the improvisation were no longer at a disadvantage compared with those who had watched it from outside. As well as their subjective impressions of the experience of the improvisation, they now shared the experience of the audience as well. The following example will illustrate this. Two 14-year-old pupils, Lindsay and Janet, were asked to show what happened when Janet, the daughter, arrived home after failing her music exam and had to break the news to her father.

(*Janet enters in a vaguely gloomy way.*)

JANET  Hullo Dad.

FATHER  (*polite interest*). Hullo. How'd it go then?

JANET  I failed.

(*Pause.*)

FATHER  (*serious, but neither annoyed nor aggrieved*). Oh, that's really too bad.

(*Pause.*)

JANET  I'm sorry.

FATHER  No, don't be sorry. It's a hard exam . . . I didn't . . . . Well, I did pass—did not fail my first grade eight. I remember . . . .

JANET  I only lost by five—I mean I only failed by five marks.

FATHER  Yes, well that's not really that bad. It's a very difficult thing. It was difficult when I took it and they've made it more so now.

The tape was played straight back and discussion centred on two things: firstly, how the daughter would approach the problem of confessing her failure; and, secondly, how the father reacted. General feeling in the group was that the father was far too soft. Lindsay disagreed, though, and said that he thought this was how his father would react. I then asked him to play the father 'tougher'. This created a problem which he solved in an interesting way.

(*Janet enters slowly, head down, not wanting to look at father.*)

JANET Hullo, Dad.

FATHER (*putting down paper he has been reading, using a pleasant and welcoming tone*). Oh, you're home. I bet it feels good to get that grade eight out of the way.

JANET (*after a slight pause, somewhat indistinctly*). I failed.

FATHER (*unbelievingly*). You what?

JANET (*even more indistinctly*). Failed.

(*Pause.*)

FATHER Your grade eight exam? Oh you're kidding.

JANET No, I failed .... I'm sorry, I just couldn't ... answer some of the questions.

FATHER All those years of playing the piano ... grade eight ... oh come on. Really that—what a waste of time and money to go and fail that one. (*His tone here is increasingly one of moral criticism rather than anger. He is putting her on the spot.*)

JANET (*trying to break out of it*). I know but—

FATHER (*cutting in*). It's the most important. You really should have studied harder for that one.

JANET (*her position very weak now*). I studied as hard as I could.

FATHER What were you doing last weekend?

JANET (*slight pause, admitting defeat*). We-ell.

The change from a rather muddled piece of work to an improvisation that showed both clarity of thought and some kind of real relationship seemed to me to have taken place far more quickly and less painfully than would have been the case if a video-recording had not been used. Lindsay discovered that moral pressure could be just as effective as anger in such a situation, but he made the discovery in an important way; he not only experienced the results on her of his behaviour in the heat of the moment, but later was able to observe his own behaviour and the way in which he achieved these results. At this point a more significant value of CCTV work became clear: Lindsay was able to see himself more or less as Janet saw him. He not only heard his own voice as she heard it, but saw posture, gesture, and facial expression as she saw them; he got the whole message of his own behaviour almost exactly as she did.

## Appendix

It is in this paralinguistic application that CCTV is clearly most valuable and three variations suggest themselves as areas for further work:

1 Concentrating camerawork on some part of the body other than the face (hands, feet, body posture).
2 Shooting a whole scene from the viewpoint of one character.
3 Playback without sound—that is, concentrating the attention of the class purely on paralinguistic features, or, if it is possible, make the video-recording without the rest of the class being present and then discussing the overall meaning of the scene with and without the soundtrack.


## Notes

1 This appendix is largely based on an article in *Young Drama* I.3 and I am grateful for permission to reproduce it here.

# Bibliography[1]

Abercrombie, David (1968), *Paralanguage* (quoted in Laver and Hutcheson, 1972).

Adland, David (1964–72), *The Group Approach to Drama*, Longman.

Allen, John (1974), 'Drama–Frill or Fundamental?', *Dialogue* 18.

Argyle, Michael (1969), *Social Interaction*, Tavistock Publications.

Bernstein, Basil (1971), *Class, Codes, and Control I*, Routledge and Kegan Paul.

—— ed. (1972), *Class, Codes, and Control II*, Routledge and Kegan Paul.

Bowskill, Derek (1973a), 'Word-Play Word-Plays Words-Play Word-Splay', *Young Drama*, Vol. 1, No. 2.

—— (1973b), *Acting and Stagecraft Made Simple*, W. H. Allen.

Brecht, Bertolt (1939), *Die Strassenszene, Grundmodell eines epischen Theaters* (translated in Bentley, E., *The Theory of the Modern Stage*, Penguin, 1968).

Creber, J. W. Patrick (1972), *Lost for Words*, Penguin/The National Association for the Teaching of English.

Doughty, Peter (1974), *Language, 'English', and the Curriculum*, Edward Arnold.

Doughty, Peter, Thornton, Geoffrey, and Pearce, John (1971), *Language in Use*, Edward Arnold.

—— (1972), *Exploring Language*, Edward Arnold.

Goffman, Erving (1955), *On Face-Work: An Analysis of Ritual Elements in Social Interaction* (quoted in Laver and Hutcheson, 1972).

—— (1959), *The Presentation of Self in Everyday Life*, Penguin.

Gordon, Chad, and Gergen, Kenneth, J. (1968), *The Self in Social Interaction*, Wiley.

Halliday, M. A. K. (1973), *Explorations in the Functions of Language*, Edward Arnold.

—— (1974a), *Language and Social Man*, Longman.

—— (1974b), 'Language as Social Semiotic: Towards a General Sociollinguistic Theory', LACUS/ALCEU Forum No. 1, Chicago.

Halliday, M. A. K., McIntosh, Angus and Strevens, Peter (1964), *The Linguistic Sciences and Language Teaching*, Longman.

Heathcote, Dorothy (1967), 'Improvisation' in *English in Education*, Vol. 1, No. 3.

H.M.S.O. (1967), *Education Survey 2, Drama*.

H.M.S.O. (1975) *A Language For Life*.

Hodgson, John, and Richards, Ernest (1966), *Improvisation*, Methuen.

Holbrook, David (1961), *English for Maturity*, Cambridge University Press.

Joseph, Stephen (1967), *Theatre in the Round*, Barry and Radcliffe.

Jourard, Sidney (1968), 'Healthy Personality and Self Disclosure' in Gordon and Gergen (1968).

Laver, John and Hutcheson, Sandy (1972), *Communication in Face-to-Face Interaction*, Penguin.

Lynskey, Alan (1974), *Children and Themes*, Oxford University Press.

Pemberton-Billing, R. N., and Clegg, J. D. (1965), *Teaching Drama*, University of London Press.

Seely, John (1971a), 'The Language of Improvisation' in *Speech and Drama* XX.2.

—— (1971b), 'Sincerity, Reality, and Fiction' in *Speech and Drama* XX.3.

—— (1974), 'Recording the Drama Lesson' in *Speech and Drama* XXIII.3.

Slade, Peter (1954), *Child Drama*, University of London Press.

Spolin, Viola (1963), *Improvisation for the Theater*, Northwestern University Press.

Stone, Gregory P., and Farberman, Harvey A. (1970), *Social Psychology Through Symbolic Interaction*, Ginn Blaisdell.

Styan, J. L. (1963), *The Elements of Drama*, Cambridge University Press.

—— (1971), *The Dramatic Experience*, Cambridge University Press.

Walker, Brenda (1970), *Teaching Creative Drama*, Batsford.

Waller, Willard (1961), 'The Definition of The Situation' (quoted in Stone and Farberman, 1970).

Way, Brian (1967), *Development Through Drama*, Longman.

Yates, Patricia, and Hornby, Robert (1974), *Ideas in Action I*, English Universities Press.

## Note

1 Reference has not been made in the above bibliography to any works that are only mentioned in Chapter 10, which is itself an annotated bibliography.